Herbert Vollmann · What lies behind it . . .!

Herbert Vollmann

What lies behind it...!

The Grail Message
Foundation Publishing Co.
Stuttgart

Translated from German. Title of the original German edition: "Was dahinter steht...!" (Copyright 1976 by Herbert Vollmann.) Produced by Verlag der Stiftung Gralsbotschaft, Stuttgart, Germany.

This paperback contains the translation according to the sense of the original German text. In some cases the word-forms of the translation can only render the meaning and contents of the original approximately. Nevertheless the reader will come to a good understanding of it, if he strives to absorb the meaning of the contents inwardly.

ISBN 3-87860-083-6

© 1977 by Herbert Vollmann, Vomperberg/Tyrol

CONTENTS

The following topics are also dealt with in the essays: The origin of the human spirit – The meaning of life – Auto-suggestion – Predestination – Faith in God – Nature-beings – Cosmic radiation – Nostalgia – Phantom-pains – The interpretation of horoscopes – Karmaic reactions – Collective crime.

FOREWORD

Behind everything stands the Will of God, moving and sustaining!

On this side, in the gross matter of this earth, we see everywhere only the ramifications, the *final* effects of this Eternal Will, Which finds expression in His immutable Laws.

For the human spirit it is now particularly stimulating and gladdening to be able to investigate and divine the *deeper meaning* of outward happenings and events; for what is real lies beyond earthly comprehension, and can be grasped only with the spiritual faculties.

This shall be attempted here. At the same time may the reader recognise one thing or another that cannot be fathomed with mere earthly knowledge, and yet represents the reality.

Vomperberg, Tyrol, August 1976

Herbert Vollmann

THE STARS AND FATE

We have heard at various times of returning evil or good currents of fate, and it may be asked in what way do they come back to their originator, and when does this happen. For here as everywhere some order must prevail which is firmly established in the plan of Creation, and which admits of no arbitrariness. Are these currents of fate controlled, and who takes part in it?

To understand these processes let us begin with the atom. The driving energy in atoms arises through minute spirit-motes which are equipped with a spiritual though *graded* power. From distant heights they stream unceasingly to us, into the Gross Material World, where they give rise to the formation of a great number of atomic species.

They are the same spirit-particles which also accumulate into heavenly bodies. Our sun is one such immense concentration of them, and in its emanation, or differently expressed, in the electro-magnetic waves which it sends out and which we call sunlight, these spirit-particles in turn are contained. This solves the enigma of what in the true sense of the word is the life-giving power of the sun's rays, without which life on earth would be impossible.

But not only the sun, everything else also sends out rays, or better said mingled radiations resulting from the various combinations of atoms among themselves. Thus the earth, the stars, rocks and plants have their specific radiations, likewise the bodies of men and animals. Natural science is only now beginning to grasp these radiations in their initial stages.

All these radiations together result in a widely-ramified,

colourful radiation-network, which in turn is linked with other radiations coming from out of the Universe.

In the midst of this vast radiation-network stands the human spirit of the earth with his wreath of radiations, which forms the antenna for the reception of radiations from out of the Universe.

What is decisive for him is how he exercises his free will during his earth-life, what radiations he draws to himself from out of the Universe, and above all how he makes use of the spiritual power continually streaming through Creation. This power is neither good nor bad, but neutral. Only by using it is man able to form his "works", through the volition of his inner perception. He needs the spiritual power as stimulus for the forming of good and bad works, which make up his *fate* (karma), and with which he remains linked until they are redeemed. Man is not capable of creating anything himself; he is only able to form by uniting already-existing individual forms. In this connection it should be noted that these works, just like everything else, send out rays and are active. They are forms which, in union with homogeneous species, give rise to incisive effects.

The activity of these works is very clearly expressed in the language through "activity-words" (verbs), for example as when a thought strikes us, hatred is nurtured in our heart or courage rises, when we take fright, arouse fear, or when envy gnaws at our heart, when we are consumed with worry, or tormented by some craving.

These are no empty phrases, but actual, even if invisible, processes, which are expressed through word-forms.

If now our fateful works emit radiations, and the stars also radiate, then it becomes clear that stars and fate are connected through radiations.

The radiations of the stars form channels in which the reactions corresponding to the nature of the radiations are guided collectively to the originator when according to the Laws of Creation they are due. "For only when it is ripe does the fruit of Fate fall" (Schiller). Evil currents of fate find their way to unfavourable radiations, and good currents of fate to favourable radiations.

If there is no homogeneous fate the channels run empty, bringing neither good nor evil. But in spite of this they still exercise an influence in that, for example, empty unfavourable channels can interrupt good reactions, and vice versa. Through the ever-changing reciprocal radiation of the stars, the most diverse effects are thus produced.

After these explanations, the real meaning of an astrological prediction is now no longer hard to understand. In so far as this is possible with the stars available for calculation today, it can of course be stated when bad or good reactions are possible, when for instance Saturn moving in the sky forms a "bad" radiation-aspect to the position of Mars in the birth-horoscope; but this is still not enough for a fully detailed interpretation. In addition, it must be determined whether any karma is actually passing through the ascertained channels. Thus the one interpreting would at the same time have to be a clairvoyant, or at least work in association with a clairvoyant, to be able to discern the fine currents of fate or the empty state of the channels.

In this connection however it should be observed that in our time the reactions, which for the most part are of an evil nature, are running at full speed, and that therefore the predictions have a considerably greater likelihood of being fulfilled. This is connected with the Cosmic Turning-Point and the Final Judgment, during which through certain radiations an acceleration is called forth in all spheres of life which crowds all redemptions closely together with regard to time, through which striking accumulations of all kinds of fateful events come about. This implies at the same time an accumulation of "hits" based only on *calculations* concerning the future, without knowing whether there are threads of fate for them.

But now in addition to all the predictions comes something else of importance: how does man receive these? In most cases he is disturbed by unfavourable predictions, his confidence, his trust, are impaired, so that even if the stellar channels are running empty, out of fear of what is coming a fulfilment is forcibly brought about which otherwise would not be there.

In the case of favourable predictions, vigilance may slacken in careless expectation of something good, which is equally harmful. Finally there is the danger of being fettered, of an inner constraint if the predictions form the basis of every single action. The inner perception is dulled, and eventually man becomes a slave of his destiny.

Therefore he should know how to assess astrological predictions aright, and on no account should he accustom himself to or make himself dependent upon them, because they are incomplete, and can always be given only in the form of what is *possible*.

Instead he should rely on the inner perception of his spirit, look to the future with calm confidence, and content himself with knowing what the stars have to do with fate: Their radiations serve to let returning effects of fate flow to him in a more concentrated form at those times which are appointed for it according to the Laws of Creation. That is to say he does indeed have the free will for decision, nevertheless he must leave the *consequences* of his decision and the *moment for the return of the consequences* to the Laws of God. He has no influence over these.

Certainly a birth-horoscope accurately calculated also gives indications for the *present time* with reference to environmental relations (upbringing, occupation, relationships with other people, liability to illness, etc.). But to form a judgment on this requires, in addition to the earthly circumstances, the psychic condition and the ethereal environment of the one born, with all the as yet unsevered good and bad threads of fate.

Thus here too the stellar calculation reveals only the possibility of a many-sided interpretation, and it is extremely difficult to discover what is real about it.

Nevertheless a limited use of the horoscope is possible. For it is conceivable that one called for it, who engages in psychic counselling, uses a person's birth-horoscope as a guide-line, in order to recognise abilities, personal disposition and possible karmaic effects in it. Together with the information from the person concerned, these can then be supplemented by the following: handwriting, the lines of the hand, shape of the head and other aids, in order to determine approximately how far the possibilities indicated in the horoscope have been realised at the time of counselling. –

Even though the stars have yet other effects, they are in everything still only participants in the great order-plan of Creation. Man as its *originator* always remains the master of his fate.

The activity of the stars thus described gives us the important recognition of *why* they can neither influence the free will of man nor exercise compulsion over him.

On the contrary, the supposed influence emanates from man himself, who in his free choice supplies the "material of fate" which the stars only return to him in the same kind, though many times increased, just as with a seed-grain multiple fruits grow for the sower.

However severe the reactions may often be, man is always in a position to protect himself against returning evil through a timely inward change for the good.

If nevertheless it one day strikes him with full force, then he should not "quarrel with fate", and above all he should not let himself be incited to commit or allow himself to be carried away by further misdeeds. Otherwise he makes his position worse and "jumps from the frying-pan into the fire", as the saying goes.

He should then remember the words of Jesus in the parable: "But I tell you, Resist not him that is evil" (Matthew 5, 39 – Lutheran Bible). If by this we understand the evil that comes back on man, then these words mean that man acts aright when he stands up to his evil fate courageously, and with trust in Divine Justice – taking up the struggle with it and living through the consequences of what he has done wrong. There are always breathing-spaces in the course of it. The stars also ensure this by periodically interrupting evil reactions with favourable radiations.

The man thus oppressed and afflicted is thereby forced to awaken spiritually, and eventually emerges strengthened from the struggle with "the power of destiny". Actually in so doing he has conquered himself, because he has overcome his faults and weaknesses. In the consequences of his deeds and thoughts he has recognised his deserved and just fate.

Let us see to it, however, that in future we do only what is good and refrain from evil, so that only good is left to the reactions of the stars. Then a kind fate will fall to our lot, which allows our spiritual development to take place harmoniously, until one day a planetary hour, thus an auspicious, fateful hour is allotted to us here on earth, in which we may recognise the Eternal Truth!

THE VISITING OF SINS UNTO THE THIRD
AND FOURTH GENERATION

The Law of Seed and Harvest, Cause and Effect, which can also be called the Law of Reciprocal Action, is a *uniform* Law for the whole of Creation, applying equally to human actions and thoughts, and determining the course of fate.

To this also pertain happenings which are designated as *chance,* with the implication of arbitrariness and blind sway.

In reality, however, they are the effects of lawful processes, which are often strange and inexplicable, because man is no longer in a position to survey and recognise the invisible connections in them.

By viewing his fate intellectually he advances no further. Extra-earthly realms are involved here, which are not accessible to the earthly intellect.

How often we say in regard to fateful events: It was an unfortunate or fortunate accident, chance willed it so, it was brought about by a series of accidents, or it was a game of chance. But the game was known, it went according to incorruptible rules, determined by the Laws of Creation.

In accordance with the same Laws, many human souls must again return to earth to make good, to redeem the sins which they once committed on earth. For earthly beginning stipulates earthly ending in accordance with the Law of the Cycle, by which the ring must close at the place where it was begun. "Thus all guilt avenges itself on earth" (Goethe), according to which the Biblical expression "to avenge" means nothing other than the working out of the Law of Sowing and Reaping.

The same Law is expressed by the Biblical words: "The

iniquity of the fathers is visited upon the children unto the third and fourth generation" (Exodus 20, 5).

The visiting does not refer to heredity. What is inherited is only purely physical. We see it for example with drug addicts and drunkards, whose children then suffer from physical defects.

But there is no spiritual heredity. Therefore the visiting refers *only* to the *karmaic reactions* of a sin which, for instance, parents commit against their children. Its effect goes on from generation to generation, until in one generation a halt is called to the necessary atonement through better recognition, and it is possible for the originator to begin with the redemption of his karma.

One such sin is when parents instill into their children that life does not continue after death, that everything is then ended. This gives rise to very far-reaching, adverse effects, especially if the offspring retain this false view, and pass it on to the grandchildren. These effects continue until in one generation the right recognition of an after-life arises, and the originator is only then able gradually to sever himself from his guilt.

The present-day conditions of moral decline in particular are rooted to a considerable extent with young and old in the fatal view that man lives only once on earth. Hence earth-life is senselessly enjoyed without consideration for one's fellow-men, and with total disregard of the responsibility placed upon man by God. Escape into narcotics and drugs, into illness and suicide, is to some extent connected with this.

At the same time no thought is given to the consequences of the reaction, and yet they take effect, here on earth or there in the beyond, regardless of human volition and thinking, which rarely accords with the Laws of Creation.

THE KINGDOM WITHIN US

This expression is often used. People also say: the Kingdom of Heaven or the Kingdom of God within us.

As to the real meaning of these words there are only vague ideas, which leave open the main questions: In what way is the Kingdom of God within man? Has it always been within us? Or does it only enter into man later, perhaps through the Word of God?

The "Kingdom within us" is closely linked with the Law of the Cycle, which can be easily observed in Nature.

The human spirit also is subject to this Law, which means that each one must return to its origin, just as the blood ever again flows back to the heart.

But where does the origin of the human spirit lie?

In the Spiritual Realm, which we call the Paradise of the human spirits, or "the Kingdom of Heaven"; there is his origin, his true home, the Kingdom of God.

Far above the Spiritual Realm is the Divine Sphere, and God Himself in His Unsubstantiality, eternally unapproachable and incomprehensible to the human spirits.

Hence the human spirit cannot bear within it anything Divine, because its origin lies much *lower,* in the *Spiritual* Realm.

It lives there as an unconscious spirit seed-grain, which is released (expelled) from Paradise, and plunges into the material substance of the World that lies below. Here the spirit awakens to full consciousness, and in natural development returns to Paradise as conscious of itself, as the "prodigal son" who has found his way back to his homeland.

The core of man, thus what constitutes the essential part of man, his spirit, is of such a kind as exists in the Spiritual Realm.

Through this he is himself a part of the Spiritual Realm, a part which he as earth-man bears within him and which is eternal, whereas all the coverings which envelop the human spirit are transient.

When Jesus was asked by the Pharisees "when the kingdom of God should come" He answered them: "The kingdom of God cometh not with observation: Neither shall they say, Lo here! or, lo there! for, behold, the kingdom of God is within you" (Luke 17, 20 and 21).

In the last Wittenberg edition of the Bible of 1545, published during Luther's lifetime, it says, "the kingdom of God is within you".

In a 1916 edition of the Bible the same words are still to be found. Later, however, Luther's translation was changed to, "the kingdom of God is in your midst".

The reason given for this by various sources was inaccuracy in the translation of the original text, and the objection that the Kingdom of God could not have been within the Pharisees because they had opposed Jesus.

Nevertheless we have seen that this is so, because spirit, and with it a part of the Kingdom of God, is in *every* human being. Except that through evil thoughts and actions this "inner kingdom" has been completely buried in some, and in others it is less strong.

But then all is not done with the "Kingdom of Heaven within us". We must earnestly strive, indeed strive with unflinching diligence, really to maintain the link with the native Luminous Fields.

We are helped to achieve this by the spiritual power that

comes from the same spiritual origin and streams through Creation.

The spirit within us, like the physical body, needs its nourishment so that it can grow into the necessary consciousness which alone makes it a complete human spirit. Just as the physical body is unable to do without water, so does the spirit need the "Water of Life", spiritual power.

It has surely been noticed already by everyone, when a strong inner shock, whether of deep sorrow or great joy, loosened the dense coverings surrounding the spirit. He then sensed for some blissful moments the nearness of this power, of which he hardly becomes conscious in everyday life.

With the help of this spiritual power, and with the gifts and abilities originally vested in him, man *would* have been in a position to let a Paradise-like condition arise on earth!

Instead of this he is suffering today from an extreme *self-estrangement*. He has estranged himself from his self, his spirit, by allowing the awareness that he has a spiritual core within him to be extinguished.

Only through a *constant* good volition shall we be able to reawaken this consciousness. Therefore let us listen within, let us hearken to the inner voice, and heed every gentle urging of the spirit towards what is beautiful and noble, every sorrow over lost spiritual values, every silent reproach of having done little or nothing yet at all to unfold to full blossom the gifts bestowed by the Creator.

When often in the midst of all darkness and all affliction, we are seized by homesickness for bygone beautiful things, for happy hours formerly experienced, for a tender, deeply spiritual mood, as may perhaps have been the case at a Christmas festival, we usually describe this today by the word: *nostalgia!*

But let us just for once examine closely with the inner

perception whether behind it there is not hidden the unquench-
able longing of the suppressed spirit that strives away from
the earth to the Eternal Fields of the Kingdom of God, of
which we bear within us the smallest part.

With the awakening of this inner longing we draw ever
more luminous rays from the Universe, which gradually loosen
and eventually altogether dissolve the self-created dark covering, so that the spirit on earth can again shine forth radiantly,
as once it did in the springtime of mankind!

THE I IN THE LANGUAGE

The sojourn of man on earth and in the beyond assists his development from an unconscious spirit-germ to a conscious ego, to a personality conscious of itself, with free will and the responsibility arising out of it.

That is the state man should strive for as soon as he has left Paradise, the Spiritual Realm, as an unconscious spirit-germ. In the throes of experiences, and through all kinds of influences assailing him, he must fight for his full spiritual maturity on his journey through the material substances of the World.

With the attainment of this goal he has completed his cycle through the World, and then returns to Paradise as a fully-conscious personality.

The development to a human spirit conscious of itself is naturally to be found in the evolution of languages. For the spirit of man also forms the language.* The more he unfolds his natural consciousness, the more is this expressed in the language, above all in the introduction and use of the word "I".

Hence it follows that, for instance, in the languages of ancient times the "I" is still little used as a single word. It is completely lacking in the verbs, and is expressed solely in their endings. Only later, with increasing development towards self-consciousness, did the "I", among some peoples, emerge, as it were, from its obscurity within the verbs, and was placed in front of them.

---

* See: "Spirit and Language", in the paperback of the Grail Message Foundation: "Knowledge for the World of Tomorrow!"

We observe the development of the human spirit to personal ego-consciousness, comprising millions of years, as a recapitulation concentrated into the childhood of present-day man. At the same time we notice that neither does the child yet use the word I, but to begin with employs its first name or a variation of it. Only later does it begin to make use of the word I, as the spirit gradually awakens to consciousness of itself.

If man reflects for once on the actual goal of his development, he will see that his ego has not remained alone. As a result of his wrong development the word "mania" has been added, as an expression of his inner condition as it manifests today, his desire for importance, and his intoxication with power.

Therefore it will not be easy for him to break free from the *egomania* prevalent today, in order to re-discover the interrupted path of natural development to the perfecting of his personality.

This involves above all the recognition that his sojourn in the earthly Gross Material World is only a *path,* and not the goal itself. Everything on earth is only a means to the end of spiritual development, to the completion of the cycle whose beginning *and* end lie in Paradise, the home of the human spirit, from which it has issued as a spirit-germ in order to return there as a complete human spirit.

ADAPTATION, BUT HOW?

A vital requirement, which Nature strictly observes, is with a few exceptions no longer known to man: *natural adaptation!* He has become incapable of mastering any longer that adaptation which furthers and ennobles his spirit.

The concept of "adaptation" has become grossly distorted, especially in the realm of human association. Whether it is a question of wrong adaptations to harmful customs in marriage and family, or of a more or less enforced adaptation to unnatural social systems.

In the realms of Nature a correct adaptation is taken for granted. Every animal, every flower, every tree adapts to the environment in which it lives – to the zone, the climate, the rays of the earth and the stars. Whether this occurs in the arctic region, in great heat, in water or in the air, everywhere we find a perfect adaptation to the natural conditions.

This automatic adaptation is only one of the many-sided effects of the *Law of Spiritual Movement!*

Man alone closes himself voluntarily to this all-animating, spirit-refreshing movement, which would also spur him on to a healthy adaptation everywhere. His earthly intellect indeed runs at high speed, but his spirit has become too lazy to open itself consciously to the spiritual power-current that moves Creation, and to make use of it in a furthering and upbuilding way.

Otherwise things would look different on earth today. Harmony and peace would spread, and joyful activity be found everywhere.

Already the Ten Commandments contain in reality enough

suggestions for a genuine adaptation, the compliance with which would bring only happiness and joy. Especially when it is recognised that to the concept of adaptation in human life there also belongs this: not to harm one's neighbour through some desire or other!

The man of today finds himself in a grave adaptation-crisis, because he is the only creature who for thousands of years has neglected to carry out that adaptation which alone really allows him to become a fully-conscious personality: *the unconditional adaptation of his spirit to the Laws of Creation!* These also include the Laws of Nature, without which research, for instance, can do nothing if it wishes to be successful. For making use of the forces of the earth, water, air and fire means nothing other than adapting oneself to the lawfulness expressed in them.

But unfortunately, in this field natural adaptation often becomes a curse, if the results of research and discoveries have to contribute to the affliction and destruction of men and animals, and to the pollution of the environment.

Anyone who now wishes to begin to concern himself with the Laws of Creation, such as the Law of Movement, the Law of the Cycle, the Law of Balance between Giving and Taking, the Law of Sowing and Reaping (the Law of Reciprocal Action), the Law of the Attraction of Homogeneous Species, or the Law of Gravity will gradually open for himself the way to an adaptation to the Will of God. For something other than the Will of God cannot be expressed in the Laws, which are His Work. And all these Laws apply not only to the realm of Nature but also to *human* life.

If man cannot or can no longer come to terms with the Old Testament ideas of God, if he is striving to form for himself a new concept of God, then he should attempt at last to begin with Creation and its Laws. He will always find in them an *imperishable* quantity (constant), an all-embracing, *uniform* whole, which offers him a firm support and does not let him waver so easily.

It can be said that Creation and its Laws make him familiar with the Language of God.

In this way man is able to master his life reliably, and to unfold his personality. There opens up to him an entirely new world-picture, in which he rediscovers himself as a creature who gets to know and to understand his origin, his goal and his task, like a revelation.

Finally he reaches that stage of development at which he recognises and *acknowledges* the Will of his God and therewith also God Himself, Who is unapproachably enthroned outside His Creation, and has woven into His Work only His Will in the form of the Laws of Creation.

This is the highest stage of adaptation to which man can attain: *the adaptation of his entire life to the Will of God, to His Laws and His Commandments.*

Then gradually he will also adapt the institutions of state and society, and all other realms, to the inflexible Laws of Creation. And such a right adaptation can bring nothing but peace, joy and ascent!

NO TIME FOR SPIRITUAL THINGS!

How little time indeed has man for any spiritual happening, although he himself, his real ego, his spirit, is a part of this happening, simply through the very fact that he originates in the Spiritual Realm. There is his Paradisal home, which he has left in the urge and longing to become conscious.

Even on earth a man who emigrates to another country does not forget his homeland, he at least thinks back to it now and then, if he is not even overcome by homesickness for the land of his earthly origin.

But he no longer knows anything of his spiritual home, which lies above in Paradise. Not even a divining of it arises within him. And yet the spirit, filled with repressed longing, is always waiting for the dark walls built around it by human guilt to be torn down, so that his gaze may become free towards the Light.

Man always has time enough for earthly things and earthly customs, but there is no time to spare for spiritual investigating and seeking, although it is actually so essential for his ascent out of this world of perishable matter, which indeed is only meant for him temporarily as a place of learning, of investigating and of development.

Man should indeed produce earthly goods and enjoy them with pleasure, but he must not place the acquisition of earthly possessions *above* spiritual gain, which alone mediates eternal values to him.

Only *these* values which he is able to acquire through genuine inner experiencing give him strong support in the beyond, firm confidence, and genuine trust in God. But the earthly values which he has acquired with the help of his intellect remain behind after death and pass away like the brain which produces the intellect.

It is just the intellect that so often stifles the rising longing of the spirit, pushing aside fruitful recognitions and experiences, declaring that it has no time for them.

May the human being in the pressure of earthly activity swing himself upwards more and more to devote sufficient time to the spiritual. It will bring the spirit multiple gain, here as well as over there in the other world, which no earthly wealth however great can outweigh.

Whether the search for the spiritual relates for example to the question of the origin of the human spirit, its task in Creation, life after death, the spiritual power by which it lives and exists, or whether it concerns its free will, its responsibility, its fate and its repeated earth-lives.

No time for spiritual things! This can only be a lazy excuse of the intellect, because by its nature it is in no position whatever to grasp spiritual things. Its field is the earthly.

The spirit, however, which is eternal, does not know this excuse. It always has time for spiritual things, as soon as and as long as it goes on striving to keep awake its longing for the Luminous Heights!

THE GREAT TRANSFORMATION

There are two main kinds of life in the whole of Creation: unconscious and conscious life.

Only through *experiencing* can the unconscious state be transformed into a conscious one. So is it also with the human spirit.

When it leaves its point of origin, men's Paradise, it is a spirit-germ which as yet has no consciousness of its own, and solely under the *urge* of becoming conscious sinks down into the Worlds of Matter in order first of all as a spirit-germ to experience *consciousness of its existence.*

The further development from consciousness of existence to *being conscious of oneself,* with the rising degrees of becoming conscious of oneself, is a long journey, with many re-embodiments (reincarnations) in *human bodies.*

For this the stage of consciousness of existence as *transition* is of course absolutely necessary, but the spirit-germ may remain there only a certain time if it does not wish to lag behind in its development, and thus in a state similar to that still to be found among some savage tribes.

The full maturity of a human spirit is equivalent to consciousness of oneself, the basis of which is *self-recognition,* that the core of man is spiritual and that his true home lies in the Spiritual Realm.

The completion of this last great stage of development should have been reached today by all human beings sojourning in the World of Matter, because the time for this is fulfilled, according to the Laws of Creation.

At the same time, with the full maturity that can grow only

out of experiencing, men would have come into possession of the true knowledge that lies only in the cognizance, without gaps, of the Laws woven into Creation by God.

On these Laws of God, or Laws of Creation, rests the order of Creation, and out of them flows all Creation-Happening. To them also belong the Laws of Nature, which are indeed partly known to science but without the latter's having recognised their origin or "original foundation", because it confines itself solely to what can be proved by the intellect.

That one cannot today speak of either a full maturity of the human spirits or a knowledge of the Laws of God is shown by the immaturity and ignorance of human beings in all that pertains to spiritual development.

With regard to their development, mankind are still between the stage of consciousness of existence and that of consciousness of oneself; in which connection it is to be noted that the animal also has a consciousness, but can never become conscious of itself, because it is of an entirely different species from that of the human spirit.

Now what is the cause of this sad standstill and retrogression in the development of mankind? *Lack of experiencing,* because only experiencing can form the bridge from the unconscious to the conscious.

Experiencing is possible for the spirit-germ only in the Worlds of Matter of Subsequent Creation, to which the earth also belongs. When it comes in contact here with the coarser and coarsest influences, there is the possibility for it to awaken out of the sleep of the unconscious, and to develop to the highest maturity.

With its *free will,* which is anchored in the spiritual species, the spirit-germ is able to choose *those* experiences which it needs in order to mature.

Yet one or several experiences at certain intervals do not suffice. The spirit must gather and assimilate many experiences and lessons in unbroken succession, until it has reached the maturity-level of the highest consciousness, of being conscious of itself, in the World of Matter.

This highest level of maturity then opens for it the gate to the Spiritual Realm, to Paradise. There it is able to perfect itself ever more in its task of being a link between the Spiritual Realm and the Worlds of Matter of *Subsequent Creation* lying below it.

It may then continue to participate in the weaving of Creation, in a furthering, upbuilding and ennobling way, because during its journey through the Worlds of Matter it became thoroughly acquainted with its sphere of work, and could gather enough experiences for its activity.

In being permitted to participate in this way lies the meaning of its existence!

Earthman must not make the mistake of applying to the Creation-Happening the *joint decision-making* striven for or demanded in the purely earthly-social realm.

In the *whole* of Creation it is exclusively the *Will of God* manifesting in the Laws of Creation Which *decides.* The human spirit, despite the fact that through its spiritual nature it is lord, so to speak, in *Subsequent Creation,* can as His creature only *participate* in that which God has already decided, but *not take part in the decision.* These are two entirely different concepts.

For it is unthinkable that man as a *creature* should decide jointly with his *Creator,* thus take part in determining what has to be done.

On earth also joint decision-making is out of place, because by virtue of his free will every human being is *himself responsible* for what he has to decide. Thus he likewise decides his fate.

If a man intrudes upon the personal environment or sphere of work of another, and wishes to make joint decisions there, he is transgressing against the decisions of the Creator, in which it is firmly established that *personal responsibility* must neither be *shifted onto* other people nor *shared* with others! Disappointments, discord and strife are the result when he does not observe this.

The expression "*joint* decision-making" does not fit into the harmonious swinging of Creation, including the earthly plane. Here, out of a wrong volition, whether due to error, misunderstanding or striving for power, man has coined a *new* expression which narrows and distorts the concept of deciding.

We obtain the right concept if we use the words *participation* and *co-operation* instead of "joint decision-making".

But then there are still other transgressions by man against the decisions of the Creator. An especially grave one was that of the *over-cultivation of the intellect.**

It is the intellect which, through wrong use, does not permit the human spirit to experience *that* which it needs for the recognition of full consciousness, because man put his intellect, which according to Divine Ordinance should be only the *instrument* of the spirit, in the place of his spirit.

The intellect arises in the frontal brain, and is active only for as long as the earthly body is animated by the spirit.

In its liking-to-know-better, the intellect does not allow living happenings to reach the spirit at all, or only weakened and distorted. Thus it prevents the undimmed advance of visible and invisible impressions and influences to the spirit.

---

* See: "Spirit, Logic and Intellect", in the paperback of the Grail Message Foundation: "Knowledge for the World of Tomorrow!"

Through the predominance of the intellect, with its paralysing and enervating pondering, man has narrowly limited his possibilities of experiencing.

He thereby closes himself to the luminous currents which he absolutely needs on earth, because these help him in the first place to be continually experiencing and vigilant.

What is happening at the present time, however, is meant to assist him in a way that is capable of violently rousing human beings of a good volition, whereby the way becomes free for a pure, unimpaired experiencing, which consciously makes full use of the supra-earthly radiation-forces, and will not as hitherto let them pass it by.

In these power-currents permeating Creation, without which there is no life, lie both help and salvation for the human spirit.

Thus even at the last moment it is given the opportunity to complete the *great transformation from an unconscious spirit-germ to a personality conscious of itself,* which it has hitherto postponed.

In his earthly garb man is unable to appreciate the magnitude and the spiritual value of this transformation. Only when he has laid aside the heavy earthly cloak, and gradually ascends to higher, more luminous fields, will there come to him a divining of what he has gained with God's gift of a conscious life.

Then his development in Gross Matter has come to an end. But in the Spiritual Realm, in Paradise, it continues steadily, without end, in ever-increasing activity and glowing, in the supreme joy of *being permitted to serve eternally* in the Luminous Kingdom of the Creator!

MORE UNDERSTANDING
FOR ONE'S NEIGHBOUR

How vital is the harmonious relationship of man to man emerges even from the Ten Commandments alone, which Moses once was permitted to mediate to men.

Many centuries later, words were again spoken on earth with the aim of making behaviour towards one's neighbours simple and natural, thus pointing the way to Luminous Heights.

"Love thy neighbour as thyself!" said the commandment of the Son of God Jesus, when He saw how envy and self-seeking had overgrown the garden of love of the soul beyond all recognition.

But however much He exerted Himself to shape man's path in the World of Matter through respect and understanding love towards his fellow-creatures into a path of continuous, un-dimmed happiness leading only through flowering gardens filled with glorious beauty, to the same extent has man closed himself to these exhortations and counsels, and simply disregarded them.

Hardly one earthman still stands *beside* the other. Distrust, envy and hatred have created gulfs which can scarcely be bridged any more, and the concept of the neighbour, as it swings in the God-willed working of Creation, has long since lost its true value and its true meaning.

There was once a time when men were still what we call balanced. They knew the Law of Balance, were living witnesses to the fact that they were allowed to take from the Table of the Lord, from the gifts which God through His

Creation graciously permits to be offered to human beings, only as much as they themselves needed. Through this not one of their fellow-men was harmed and taken advantage of, not one was caused suffering through selfish desires. It was a uniformly-radiating streaming of human activity, which was moved in regular pulsation by the Law of Balance in giving and taking.

Today man in relation to his Creator is only one who takes, or rather one who demands, ruthlessly seizing everything he can lay hands on in his selfishness, without showing even the slightest gratitude as a minute gift in return. In addition to this men no longer open themselves to the animating streams from above, but willingly absorb the influences of the Darkness, and pass them on in various ways.

And over all the darkness of human egomania stand in golden radiance the words: "Love thy neighbour as thyself!" Pure and clear, these words float above mankind. Yet only rarely does a light, delicate ray grope its way to them out of the depths, seeking connection and pleading for strength to overcome the individual's own ego, for a just understanding of his fellow-man, who like him is seeking for the Truth.

Man however must concern himself with his neighbour, must learn to respect and understand him as a part of the same spiritual species, as a fellow-creature who has the same path and the same goal: the Spiritual Home, Paradise.

To this end observation of his fellow-men can be very useful to him. Simply because in them he can discover, and in recognising reflect upon the faults which human nature out of its free volition, thus because of its own guilt, has nurtured outside Paradise in the World of Matter. In view of the ego-stressed character of most men, however, there is always the danger that the observing is not done objectively, and usually becomes a personal comparing, with the result that the one making the comparison imagines himself to be above the faults discovered in the other. According to the words of Jesus, he then certainly sees the mote, the lesser fault, in his fellow-man, whereas he does not notice the beam, the *same* but greater fault, in himself.

On the other hand, impartial, objective observation requires nothing more than for once leaving the ego-stressed standpoint and trying to put oneself in the place of the "object", in this case of the fellow-man, *entering with one's soul into* his thoughts and actions, and not carpingly and critically probing or dissecting with the earthly intellect.

In this connection it may prove a useful hint for the recognition and understanding of the merits and faults, that men have distorted just what was meant to distinguish them. If for instance a man was meant to stand out through *courage,* then with a wrong volition he will pervert it to *lack of courage* and *cowardice. Grace* becomes *vanity, humility* changes to *arrogance, kindness* to *harshness,* and a deep *inner* and thought-life turns into one of excessive *feeling* and *superficiality.* Above all, those qualities and those abilities are distorted through which a human being should be exemplary; and in the distortion every good quality has a definite fault as its opposite. Thus grace and charm change to vanity, and not perhaps to cowardice, which manifests as the opposite of courage.

All these opposites were forcibly brought about through the guilt of the human spirits. They could never have arisen if the human spirits had not forsaken the right path to the Light. Only the evil volition of men thus created, in opposition to God, the Darkness which embraces all faults and weaknesses.

If now in the course of these reflections the question arises in our soul: "What then have I distorted that was meant to make me into a serviceable and useful building-stone in the mighty structure of Creation?", then in this first step towards reflection the beginning of the road to self-recognition has been found. To him who treads it will soon be shown the right understanding of his fellow-man, who like himself bears within him the longing for the Luminous Heights, for the Spiritual Home.

The sooner this longing for the Light unfolds to full greatness and strength through the harmonious working together of all good human spirits, the sooner will a reflection of Paradisal beauty then arise on the hitherto so misused earth.

WHAT IS HAPPINESS?

In world literature there are a considerable number of writings and books in which an attempt is made to show men the way to happiness. On picking up such promising books and trying to delve into their contents, it can be noted in the great majority of cases that by happiness is meant only a very ordinary earthly advantage in social and material respects.

Above all people strive to achieve a position which, apart from satisfying the need for prominence, brings with it earthly riches. They have thereby attained their goal on the way to happiness, which in this case leads only as far as the earthly senses and feelings are able to perceive it.

It is understandable and commendable if a person wishes to work his way upwards, if he strives to establish a sound material foundation for his earthly existence. But in achieving this goal he still has by no means attained to happiness, that real and true happiness which has its beginning only in grasping and experiencing spiritual events, and yet at the same time permits life on earth to be fully and wholly enjoyed, indeed which alone makes it possible to savour earthly pleasures in pure joy to the full.

In Creation the development always takes place from above downwards. Hence "earthly happiness" too is only a result of the supra-earthly inner perceiving of happiness that can be consciously experienced already on earth.

But it cannot be attained either through intellectual training or by *auto-suggestion*.

For it is wrong to believe that the power to influence lies in man himself, that he is in a position to cure himself of illnesses by his own power, and to be himself the architect of his own happiness. True, each man is the architect of his happiness. But from whence does he draw the material to build with?

The idea of auto-suggestion is in opposition to God, Who alone is the Power from Whose Radiation Creation came into being, and with it also man. But after it has come into being the creature "man" can actually continue to exist only through the Power coming forth from God. With this recognition nothing remains of any auto-suggestion arising from one's own power! On the contrary, man is in every respect dependent on the Spiritual Power streaming into Creation from God; he must submit to it, otherwise it will turn against him and bring about his downfall.

And this spiritual power is the material that man needs to build his happiness.

He can consciously establish connection with it at any time. The key to this is an inner perception filled with longing to let himself be completely permeated by this power, to surrender to it with wide-opened soul, unreservedly, without any selfish desires whatever. Then it flows into him in the simplest way, with no need for a great effort. Not for anything in the world would man ever again be without this conscious receiving of the power, when once he has recognised that only this being linked with it is his supreme happiness, wherever he may find himself in the measureless expanses of Creation.

Surely everyone has already met with this power, when the soul is awakened by some strong experience, whether it be a deep sorrow or great joy. Then for some moments it senses the nearness of this all-animating power, of which it is not conscious in everyday life.

Where this inner perception still lies slumbering beneath a thin covering, it can be awakened and furthered; where it has

36

already awakened man can strengthen it and let it glow even more through regular attunement in prayer to the Power coming from God.

There are two kinds of prayer: First the prayer which instantaneously arises out of an upwelling inner perception, and only then can be clothed in words; and then the prayer in which words are first arranged and then, reacting on the spirit, release the inner perception, thereby giving the prayer that direction which is willed by the words. Hence there are, to put it briefly, prayers without words and prayers with words. The former are of greater value, for in them the spirit can unfold freely and without constraint and is not tied to words, which can be formed and received only with the help of the earthbound intellect, thereby making a certain limitation of the inner perception unavoidable.

Nevertheless, during their sojourn in the World of Matter the human spirits cannot do without the prayer that is clothed in words, because just here the spirit needs the most varied impressions for higher development, among which the prayer formed in words ranks as one of the first. It is therefore not immaterial what words are used in such prayers and how they are arranged, for words are something living and motivating in the working of Creation. As man uses them, arranges them into sentences, as he pronounces them, so does he also form with them a part of his fate for himself!

Therefore the more the words of a prayer resound in the innermost being of man, the greater also is the possibility thereby — and without undue effort or auto-suggestion, thus in a natural way — of rousing the inner perception, which as an attribute of the spirit is incisive for man's fate in a very special way.

Abd-ru-shin, Author of the Work "In the Light of Truth", The Grail Message, has among other things given men two prayers* which fulfil everything in this regard. In their simple and thus so effective way they speak directly to the soul. They are a strong aid in the evoking and growth of that longing which is necessary for the complete and gapless connection with the helping and furthering Rays from the Power of God.

How light it must become around a human spirit, how liberated it will feel when it surrenders completely to the words given to us as morning prayer:

"Thine am I, Lord! To Thee alone in gratitude I dedicate my life; accept this my volition in Thy Grace, and grant me the help of Thy Power this day! Amen."

For him who absorbs these words within, who receives them with a live spirit, the day's work will be blessed from early morning till late at night. They will constantly resound in him like a gentle exhortation or a quiet, serene happiness. There is a sacred power surging and weaving in these words, and whoever absorbs the words with his spirit also absorbs the power.

He will not always immediately succeed in obtaining connection through this prayer, because it depends on the depth of the inner perception with which it is experienced. But however weak that may be, through constant awakening it will eventually become so strong and victorious that it will open the way for the blissful experiencing of the wonderful Power from the Creator's Fountain of Life. Then even the weakest person can unfold to full strength within a short time, if he does not weaken in regular inward perception of the words of this morning prayer.

As in the morning and during the day, so also in the evening the same power is available for connection with man, if he longs for it. He is given help for this by the evening prayer:

---

* Prayers, The Grail Message Foundation.

"O Lord, Who art enthroned above all the Worlds, I beseech Thee that I may rest in Thy Grace this night! Amen."

Sleep will have an invigorating, refreshing and calming effect on a human being who takes over the experience of this prayer with him into another world, a dream world, which however is not a dream one at all, but only appears as such because it cannot be perceived with the earthly senses. We therefore refer to it as transcendental, and every human spirit can cross its threshold when the earthly brain is put to rest through sleep, and thus remains disconnected.

The evening prayer is to help towards this. During sleep the human spirit can come in contact still much more closely and lastingly with various power-currents, and even receive spiritual warnings, or also sudden solutions to certain questions and problems. In reality the natural rest at night is like this: Only the earthly brain, the intellect, sleeps; the spirit however is awake, and blissfully yields to the strengthening influences, provided no excessive intellectual activity makes itself felt disturbingly and obstructively across and beyond the threshold of sleep. But the possibility of preventing this is given by the deep inner perceiving of the evening prayer.

Such prayers lead man to the refreshing Spring of Living Water, which need only be tapped in order to drink from it, and then to regain health in soul and body, indeed completely so. The awakening human spirit, even the poorest and weakest, can receive strength from these prayers to work its way upwards, spiritually and in an earthly sense, to a height never yet known, where it will find that for which all true seekers have already yearned for a long time: "supreme happiness" — which is equivalent to fulfilment of the vow:

"Thine am I, Lord! To Thee alone in gratitude I dedicate my life! Amen."

HEAVENLY MELODY

An inconceivably long time ago, a great train of bright little flames went forth from their Eternal Home, where a delicate breath of spring had only just awakened them out of a deep sleep. Many a luminous hand was raised in blessing, as though in a last greeting, and loving, kindly glances followed after them.

The bells of Paradise were ringing as they departed, and even at the last moment they caught this silver-clear tone, and cherished it deep in their young hearts.

Then the little points, whirling merrily, sank into the world-embracing depths. –

The time came when these delicate little flames had blossomed forth in purity into human spirits, and in the blossoming there mingled a faint note from far, faraway lands, which touched the strings of their hearts like gentle hands, awakening that tone which had sounded so beautiful to them as they departed, and which they had quietly received into their innermost being.

Then they were seized by a vehement urge; for they knew the sweet sound of home, and soon their strings resounded more fully, and their song grew into a melody filled with longing.

That was the time when planet earth still revolved in luminous orbits, and when fresh heavenly dew fell on it each day.

Then came a day when that longing-filled ringing became fainter, weaker. Discords were heard. At first here and there, and then they filled the Universe. Alarmingly the jubilation of the voices faded, soon the great chorus had fallen silent. No echo could be heard any longer in the Dome of Heaven. The holy singing of earthmen had died away. –

Man had voluntarily created for himself a very effective trap. Following the urge for development, he descended from Paradise into the material substance of Subsequent Creation, but he forgot his origin and was caught in the World of Matter. Thus he could no longer make anything of the urging and exhorting within his heart.

In place of the longing, the yearning for Truth and Eternal Life, the greater part of mankind put the craving for earthly things, the desire for pleasures of the lowest kind. When the Heavenly did for once knock warningly under a dense cover, they sought to drown it in the earthly.

One frenzy after another seized the human spirit. Had some poison paralysed it that it could so forget the song of its Spiritual Home? Was it no longer able to recall that wondrous sound, which so strangely makes the heart tremble in secret joy?

When people far from their earthly homeland meet with others of their countrymen, the joy of seeing each other again is often endless, and they are proud of their earthly country. But do they then no longer know that they call yet another Homeland their own, one much more beautiful, much more flourishing? Why do they never speak of *this,* their original Home, Paradise, why do they not rejoice together over it when they meet down here on the earth-plane during their long journey through the Worlds?

Has the sublime song of Heaven then grown so completely silent in the hearts of men? Does not its melody after all still secretly sing and ring, where seeking men on their long journey truly long for it?

The yearning that slumbers in the core of the soul is only

veiled. Does man not mark how the unquenched longing is constantly knocking and exhorting, when he sets out on his travels, when he wishes to journey through the lands, across the seas, when he climbs the mountain peaks, or when inexplicable restlessness comes over him in the hurly-burly of everyday life?

If he bursts these coverings with the purity of true yearning, then he is instantly connected with the eternal power of the spirit. On the path of this connection happiness quietly comes to him, a new great hope dawns in his heart.

He who can constantly keep the connection here on earth has succeeded in mastering life, he is gripped by the great love which is always anxious that his fellow-man should also find the impetus upwards to the Blessed Fields.

But he who seeks the true yearning seeks also atonement, the liberation of himself from all the guilt of past earth-lives. He therewith obliterates the traces of wrong paths which he had followed, and achieves already on earth a high degree of spiritual consciousness.

Thus man will then be firmly anchored in earth-life, and yet able to draw from the full Fount of Heaven. And the more he draws, the more alive becomes that healthy idealism which, within natural limitations, always creates lasting spiritual values, thus building a golden ladder upon which his spirit may finally enter Paradise.

What a miracle will then take place! Unconscious little spirit-sparks went forth from Paradise, and they will return as personalities conscious of themselves; they had already been in the Kingdom of God before, and yet they can see and experience it only after they have allowed their longing for the complete understanding of the Laws of Creation to mature far from home, after there is bestowed upon them, with the attainment of full consciousness, at the same time the knowledge that they are allowed to exist eternally.

Do you hear how an invisible hand glides over the golden strings of the Heavenly Harp, and how more and more loudly it rings and sings the pure, sublime melody, so that the sound may awaken the longing of your spirit, and blessed recollections rise up from the depths? Once more you can so fan your yearning with it that it may burst into flame, scorching everything base that holds you down, and luminous rays may strike your soul.

Then after a long, long time the gates of the Blessed Lands from which you once, slumbering, took the first step will be opened again. You will return on that path by which *those* human spirits may come who did not forget that bell-clear Heavenly Song, and let its last note, which they caught even as they were departing, resound in a jubilant chord.

Therefore make room within yourselves for the true longing, and free yourselves from all petty considerations. May what is great and pure be your wish and goal eternally!

THE SECRET OF GRAVITY

The problem of gravity has indeed always been a fascinating and mysterious one, and the search for a solution is still of importance also for the present time. In the forefront of this search is the neutralisation of gravity.

Isaac Newton (1642–1727) went into the problem of gravity very deeply. It is said that he was prompted to do so by an apple falling from a tree. The idea came to him that, like the earth, all bodies might have an attracting quality. He expressed this in his Law of Gravity (Gravitation). In this law the effects were indeed understood and mathematically established, but the question of the *nature* of gravity remained open.

The force with which an object is attracted by the earth is assumed to be that of gravity. As a result of this force all bodies fall in the direction of the earth's centre. If their fall is impeded by some obstruction, they exert a pressure on the latter which is described as weight.

If we wish to fathom the nature of gravity, we must look for a new way, which however cannot be followed "from below upwards", from the proximity of the earth into cosmic space. After only a short distance this would necessitate a halt at the earthly gross material boundary.

The direction of research must lead from above downwards. In this direction there is only one possible solution. All forces and force-fields manifesting in the World of Matter (i.e. in Subsequent Creation) and constantly renewing themselves have their origin in *one* power alone: *spiritual power*, with its various *gradations*. It is the *root* of all forms of energy!

Now the origin of this one power must not be sought on

earth and in its surroundings, but outside of Subsequent Creation, the Material World. This calls for a step upwards, over and beyond the earthly boundary, in order to come to reality, which also offers the solution to the coming about of gravity.

In any progressive research, realms that lie outside the known five senses must be included today in order to advance. Indeed we are unconsciously doing this already. For the discovery and application of physical laws is nothing but the acknowledgement of that invisible power which gives rise to these laws.

Therefore it should not be too difficult to envisage a power that comes from heights which are lighter and more luminous than Subsequent Creation.

These Luminous Heights are in the Spiritual Realm which lies above Subsequent Creation, and at whose lowest boundary is to be found men's Paradise.

The currents emanating from a power-centre in the Spiritual Realm force their way over the boundary of the Spiritual Realm, and flow through the parts of Creation lying below it.

To avoid erroneous conceptions, it should be pointed out that these spiritual currents *are not God Himself*, perhaps in the sense of pantheism, but they come only out of the *Radiation* of God. That is an important difference.

Now as soon as these currents have been forced across the boundary of their origin they have, through the magnetic attraction-power peculiar to them, an attracting effect on their alien, non-spiritual surroundings.

On all the animistic, ethereal and gross material planes lying below the Spiritual Realm, these currents on their way downwards attract small particles of these planes from the *loose* substance existing on each one and envelop themselves with them, whereby the radiation changes each time. In the course of this the initially uniform currents divide into innumerable tiny

45

spirit-motes or spirit-particles. In addition the loose substance attracted from the particular plane is simultaneously compressed, which in turn causes it to become heavier and sink further.

We observe the same lawful happening in a different form in the earthly, when the loose substance of mist condenses on bare copper cables under high voltage, or when in the purification of gases the loose particles of dust contained in them are attracted to the high-voltage field of electrodes, thereby forming a denser substance.

Finally the spirit-motes, equipped with several coverings, pass from the Ethereal World, the beyond, into the Gross Material, and here give rise to the formation of elementary particles. The atoms made up of these combine into numerous molecules, and thus constitute the material substance of this world, which through the spirit-motes in reality contains spiritual power, thus "energy". But mark well, this spiritual power is but the lowest gradation of the spiritual, and therefore a species different from the human spiritual, which among other things has a greater power of attraction.

In this attracting, compressing and sinking is expressed what we call the Law of Gravity, which manifests in the same way throughout all Subsequent Creation. It is called Subsequent Creation because it took form subsequent to the Spiritual Creation. It is a coarse reflection thereof.

Expressed differently, this means: The distancing of the enveloped spirit-particles from the spiritual power-centre in the Spiritual Realm brings about the beginning of the Law of Gravity. In this connection the extent of the distance depends on the heaviness of the enveloped spirit-particles. The heavier they are, the further they must distance themselves from the magnetic power-centre of the Spiritual Realm, with which they always remain connected by way of radiation, whatever the distance.

In accordance with the Law of Gravity, on its journey from Paradise to the earth, man's spirit-germ must also envelop itself with the respective loose species of the intermediate planes through which it passes, right down to the earthly gross material body as the outermost of the coverings. The finer coverings form the soul, with the human spirit as core. Without these coverings as transitions it would not be in a position to enter the earth-plane and to live and work there.

From all this it emerges that the spiritual, as soon as it is freed from its coverings, must return to the Spiritual Realm, which is not subject to the heaviness known to us. Just as the human spirit is able to enter into Paradise only when it has severed the last of its alien coverings. –

Through the attraction of the power streaming from the Ethereal World into the Gross Material World arises the condition which we designate as gravity, in that the power compresses finely-distributed particles of gross material substance into matter, which sinks because of the heaviness thus produced.

But likewise all the particles of substance that lie between the World of Gross Matter and that of Fine Matter are borne along by the power streaming at a uniform rate as it penetrates into the World of Gross Matter, and presses them downwards in the direction of the earth.

Accordingly the idea that the earth as a very large mass must have an attracting influence on smaller masses is only one possibility. But it could equally well be that in reality the *streaming-in of the radiation-power from the cosmos,* and with it the pressing towards one another of the separate masses through this power-current, *is the cause of gravitation!* This obviously effects the pressing downwards of matter in the direction of the earth.

Thus also a pendulum would not necessarily be drawn

downwards through the attraction-power of the earth, but through the pressure of rays coming from above.

In 1959 the suggestion was made at the International Congress on Satellites and Rockets that the definition of the concept of gravitation (gravity) should be altered, to the effect that no longer should the attraction-power of the earth but rather the *repulsion-power* of the cosmos be accepted as the cause of gravitation. This opinion already comes nearer to the explanation given here.

Nor must we forget that the power described was in existence even *before* the earth came into being. Consequently the earth has only issued from this power, and therefore cannot be the origin of this power but only its product, upon which the superior power continues to stream and exert pressure.

In the years 1912 and 1913 the decrease in the supposed radioactive radiation of the earth at increasing heights was to be measured by means of rising balloons. In the course of this, people were astonished to find a very intense *increase* in the radiations instead of the expected *decrease*. These radiations, however, did not come from the earth but out of the cosmos! Thus *ultra-radiation* was discovered, a cosmic *radiation* not known until then, with a very high power of penetration.

This cosmic radiation is constant, that is permanent and unchanging. In it occur particles with extraordinarily strong *energies,* which can reach any place whatsoever on the surface of the earth from all directions!

Is it not then obvious that, in this energy-invested cosmic radiation which penetrates into the earth's atmosphere from the depths of the Universe, we suspect ramifications of the currents of enveloped spirit-particles?

It is they which form the elementary particles whose core is energy, thus spiritual power, which presumably in the disintegration of radium manifests in the gamma rays as electromagnetic radiation.* Only this energy, together with the animistic forces of Nature, animates and moves gross material substance, which in itself is without life!

In this cosmic radiation could also be found the key to the opening up of new energies!

Man never has the power or the strength to neutralise the whole power of gravity working in Subsequent Creation. On the other hand, it will at some time later be possible for him, through the wise use of the Creation-Laws, to bring about a weightlessness on earth in *limited* cases.

In so doing he will logically follow the reverse way, and will have to loosen and refine the previously dense, united particles of substance. An indication of what direction the search could take in this is given us by the obvious application of the example of a hot-air balloon. Here the molecules of air are heated, and thereby driven apart. The heated air is not as heavy as the atmosphere outside, and thus allows the balloon to rise. This sinks back to the earth when the same density, or rather heaviness, as that of the outside air is reached again inside through cooling off. For density and heaviness have a causal connection.

Certainly the peoples of ancient, bygone cultures had more knowledge of cosmic forces than we have today. Ancient traditions tell of the neutralisation of gravity in men and objects. In the case of large constructions it is said to have been possible to move the heaviest stones into place without effort. In this connection we recall, for example, the stone blocks of the pyramids, or the massive squared stones of the Inca buildings, weighing up to 200 tonnes. Although there are

---

* See: "The Secret of Atomic (Nuclear) Energy", in the paperback of the Grail Message Foundation: "The World, as it could be!"

enough theories about the building methods of those days, it has still to this day remained completely unexplained just how the stone blocks were moved and fitted together.

In the book *"Lao-Tse"* (2nd Edition, German), one of the book-series of the Grail Message Foundation, we find on page 250 the following sentence in the description of the building of the Temple: "Precious stones from distant quarries were brought along with the aid of animistic helpers."

In the volume *"Ephesus"* of the same book-series it says on page 71 (2nd Edition, German): "While the women were engaged in preparing the meal and tending the animals, the men fetched trees from the forests to build their dwellings, hauling them along with the powers of giants. Hjalfdar knew how to summon and make use of special forces, so that the building of their dwellings advanced rapidly."

In Atlantis, too, the nature-beings helped with heavy work through their colossal powers (Atlantis, pages 20 and 21, *"Past Eras Awaken"*, Vol. II, German).

What kind of powers could these have been, which long, long ago were *consciously* used to transport heavy stones and timber, and in other heavy work? Apart from mechanical aids, one involuntarily thinks in this connection of the neutralisation of gravity, or rather of a counteraction to gravity through the use of certain forces of Nature. To accept this is by no means so far-fetched today, in this age of atoms and radiations.

There is a direct reference to gravity in the book, *"From Past Millennia"* (3rd Edition, German, Vomperberg/Tyrol, and Stuttgart), in a prophecy thousands of years old, which points to the present time and the near future. There it says: "Age-old wisdom which, foreseeing, sang of this time is becoming truth. Only now does man grasp the treasures of the earth, and how to apply them to bring blessing. He is learning anew to control the powers of the Universe. – Man discovers afresh the eternal Laws of Nature. Through wise instruction he is learning to neutralise the gravity of bodies. To what is perfect he gives new forms, everything strives upwards."

Some attempts to neutralise the mysterious power of gravity have also been made in more recent times. By evoking a certain vibration, by producing anti-gravitational fields and screening devices, through a metal alloy which renders the invisible cosmic radiations ineffective in a certain direction, or by electro-gravitation. There is also mention of laser beams, which could be used to neutralise gravity.

In the end all attempts to neutralise gravity on earth are probably based on effecting certain structural changes in the elementary particles of the atoms.

Already in *1927 Abd-ru-shin*, Author of The Grail Message, *"In the Light of Truth"*, explained in the journal *"Der Ruf"* *("The Call")*, numbers 5, 6 and 7, the coming-into-being and effect of the spiritual power-currents which give rise to gravity. His explanations were published again later in the book *"Fragenbeantwortungen"* (1953, Vomperberg/Tyrol and Stuttgart; published in English as *"Questions and Answers"* in 1972).

On the basis of this revolutionary Grail Knowledge there arises a totally different concept of the cause and effect of the mysterious power of gravity, a concept which has been rendered here in broad outline to provide a *stimulus*.

Progressive science and research can accordingly proceed from entirely different assumptions, resulting from the *Law of Gravity* in relation to the no less important Creation-Laws of *Reciprocal Action* (Cause and Effect) and of the *Attraction of Homogeneous Species*.

Undreamed-of progress can be made with these new recognitions *when the time is right!*

WHAT IS TIME?

With Creation there also came into existence space and time. Nothing in it is spaceless and timeless. Therefore in the whole of Creation there is a concept of space and time. For Creation is a work, and as such limited. To this work belongs inseparably that time in which spaces have formed.

Whereas Creation came into being only progressively, that is by stages in Creation-planes, the Divine Kingdom lying above it has always been there, because it is inseparably connected with God, the Prime Source of all life. But God is from eternity to eternity, without beginning and without end.

The concept of the Eternity of God is inconceivable to the human spirit. But the Work of God, Creation, which issued from His Radiation with the Words "Let there be Light", can be grasped by the spirit of man, and therefore also the concept of space and time pertaining to Creation.

Creation comprises the *Spiritual Realms,* in the lowest of which the human spirit has its origin, and the Creation formed in the image of the Spiritual Realm, *Subsequent Creation.* To this belong the divisions of the *Ethereal World,* which we call the beyond, and of the *World of Gross Matter,* to which our earth belongs.

A faint inner urge causes the unconscious human spirit-germs to leave the Spiritual Realm, so that in lower-lying planes or Worlds of Matter they will achieve consciousness of themselves in the struggle for existence, namely through the foreign influences assailing them.

Even though there is one concept of space and time for the whole of Creation, it nevertheless forms differently on each plane of Creation, according to the nature of the plane. At the same time the concept of space and time becomes narrower with the increasing distance from the Spiritual Realm, through the ever-increasing density of the region concerned. Linked with this is the ever-decreasing ability to absorb experiences.

This is the reason why there is no absolute, that is no independent concept of space and time in the whole of Creation. Space and time cannot exist by themselves alone, they must always stand in relation to things which are in space, as for example the stars in the universe.

This is also expressed in *Albert Einstein's* general theory of relativity. It explains, for instance, that everything in the universe is interdependent; there is nothing absolute in it, everything has a relation, that is a connection with everything else.

From this we can further deduce that in the final analysis the whole of Creation is dependent on the Creator Himself.

Hence if God were ever to withdraw His Work, then the condition would again be as it was before Creation.

The concept of time thus depends in each case on the individual planes of Creation, and man must inwardly perceive it in different ways according to the plane on which he sojourns, or with which plane he as an earthman is linked.

On earth for instance, because of the density of his brain, man needs the longest period of time to receive and live through a number of impressions. In the beyond the period of time for this is already significantly shorter because here the brain, from which thinking and intellect develop, no longer exists, and only direct experiencing in the inner perception of the spirit is still decisive.

Therefore the human spirit experiences the ethereal time-concepts of the beyond differently from the earthly gross material ones. This difference is shown also in mediumistic messages. As a result of the accentuated over-development of the day-brain (large brain) for thousands of years, it is rarely possible to apply ethereal, supra-earthly conceptions of time to the earthly in such a way that, for example, in the case of predictions the earthly time of fulfilment can be accurately specified.

We experience the difference in time also in dreams, when during sleep the connection between soul (the spirit with its finer coverings) and physical body is loosened. Then a whole lifetime can unroll before our inner eyes in seconds or minutes.

In the Spiritual Realm itself the experiencing in a single earth-day is then as great as on earth in a thousand years.

On this ratio is based also the statement of time in the Revelation of *John*, which was given from a high spiritual standpoint. The earthly periods of time are expressed in "spiritual" days. When it says: "three days and an half" (11, 11), this means approximately 3,500 earth-years. This is the length of time between the earth-life of *Moses* and the present Cosmic Turning-Point. In the German Lutheran version the same earthly time is rendered in another passage of the Revelation by the description: "a time, and two times, and half a time" (12, 14).

But man has lost the knowledge of these eternal things. In place of the inner perception, which alone is able to maintain the connection with the origin of the human spirit, he put the all-questioning intellect.

He therewith suppressed the true inner perceiving of time which he brought with him from his spiritual homeland. The real concept of time was pushed aside, because it cannot be grasped intellectually.

Through this also the many philosophical teachings, which in spite of all their sagacity are not in a position to recognise the ultimate meaning of time, because it is of a spiritual nature, have hitherto proved unavailing.

Unconsciously modern man indicates the loss of the true time-concept when he says "he has no time". By this he demonstrates not only the earthly lack of time, but also the want of a higher understanding of time.

The *natural* narrowing-down of the concept of time, which results from the distancing from the Spiritual Realm, must not mislead man into covering the spiritual time-concept with earthly time-concepts.

We do indeed need the concept of time bound to the earthly as an aid for the passing of events, for progress and order on earth, but over and above this transient arrangement of time into years, months, weeks and hours, we must not forget the imperishable value of "time" which can be grasped only with the inner perception of the spirit.

How small in comparison is the perceptive faculty of the intellect, which belongs to the earthly brain. It is no longer capable of grasping even the happening in the millions of years of the earth's development. This is possible for the spirit alone.

When the spirit really bestirs itself we sense very well that there is yet another concept of time than the earthly one.

We can also say that time appears to uns according to how we move inwardly. In this connection the ability and strength of receiving and experiencing, which depends on the maturity of the spirit, forms the measure for the passing of our time.

How often have we already experienced in our earth-life that the days were much too short and time seemed to fly past.

On the other hand there is also standstill and retrogression if a wrong volition of the intellect will not allow the soul to soar upwards.

This phenomenon of different perceptions of time has been under investigation for some time. In the course of this it was established that man also has an "inner clock", a "soul clock" which often does not agree with the earthly clock.

It is known, for example, that with the young the inner perception of time is extended, whereas with older people there is the prevailing inner sensation that time is moving ever faster. Or let us think of the different experiencing of time on our holidays, when the first days pass more slowly, those in the middle normally, and the last ones much too quickly.

Speed also, the relationship between distance and time, gives rise to different inner sensations of time. According to Einstein time is not something absolute. To measure it a standpoint, a reference system, is always needed. This can be a railway train travelling at a *constant* speed, in which we are sitting. A train travelling alongside us gives the impression that it is standing still. But if the other train is travelling more slowly, we have the inner sensation that our train is travelling faster. If, however, the other train travels faster, then we think we are going more slowly. Thus three different impressions during a *constant* speed of our train!

Not only has man an inner or rather a biological clock. It is also to be found in Nature; but there it is moved by other currents of power. It determines for example the exact beginning of the flights of migratory birds in autumn from northern to southern latitudes.

Sometimes the precision of the biological clock becomes disastrous, as in the case of a species of wild geese whose habitat is in the steppes of Western Siberia. Owing to some kind of environmental influences they have shifted their fixed quarters further south. Their inner clock, however, has not reacted to this change of place. With unfailing precision it drives the geese at the same time as always to set out for their winter quarters, which lie 3,500 kilometres away in India.

But it happens too early, because in the more southerly region the geese start their moulting season later, and are not yet in a condition to fly when the great migratory excitement seizes them and it is time for departure.

What do the geese do now? At the time appointed by the biological clock, they set out *on foot* in vast numbers. Thus in about ten days they travel approximately 150 km, until they reach a lake on which they can recuperate. Meanwhile their feathers have grown so far that only now can the normal flight proceed over the remaining distance. During their march on foot they suffer great losses through exhaustion and beasts of prey. –

But let us return to the explanation of the original concept of time. Man has lost it, and this loss is particularly marked in the inversion of standpoints. Earthman regards himself as the static point, in that he lets time pass him by. He speaks of times which change, and he believes that time moves on.

However, if time has existed from the beginning of Creation, if the human spirit issues from the eternal time and can return thither again, then it is not possible for time to move past him.

Reality shows an entirely different picture, which compels us to change our thinking: Time stands still! However we, the human beings, hurry towards it, move within it. For time is unchangeable and intransient. Only the forms change, just as the spirit of man always remains the same, whereas the forms of his physical body change continually.

Just as in general the entire Subsequent Creation is subject to an unceasing "dying and coming into existence", and only the Laws that bring this about are eternally the same.

Gottfried Keller divined the reality when he said in his poem, *"Time standeth still"*:

Time moves not, it standeth still,

We pass on through it.

This verse, which could never be properly explained, will now be better understood by us. And another verse in the same poem strikes us:

A drop of morning dew sparkles

In a ray of sunlight;

A day can be a pearl

And a century nothing.

This could be a comparison between the experiencing in higher planes in the time of one earth-day, which is like a pearl, and the experiencing on earth during a century. –

Time is closely linked with spiritual Light-Power which, coming from the highest starting-point of the Primordial Spiritual Realm, fills all the spiritual parts of Creation lying below it, and thence radiates into the World of Matter, into Subsequent Creation, as well.

Thus also outside its spiritual homeland, Paradise, the human spirit moves in this Power, which in time is eternal. He swims in it, so to speak, becomes more or less strongly conscious of it, depending on the degree of his ability to receive impressions and experiences, and draws from this Power the eternal values it holds in readiness. He is even able *already on earth* to find the experience of Truth in this Power, because it comes from the Truth.

True time therefore is also eternally the same in the past, present and future, because it rests in the Spiritual Power which streams to us out of Eternity, and knows no earthly limitations.

In earthly life, on the other hand, past, present and future are perceived separately in the context of time and space, and only a fraction of the wealth of spiritual happening in these three sections of time can be experienced by earthmen. This is due to their dense material covering, which brings with it narrowness of comprehension.

The spiritual power indelibly records every experience and happening in the great Book of Creation, and preserves it. Nothing of it is lost, and it is possible to make proclamations from it at any time.

We find the best examples of this in the works *"From Past Millennia"* (German) and in *"Past Eras Awaken"* (German), as well as in the accounts of the Forerunners (The Grail Message Foundation Publishing Co., Stuttgart).

In all these books it is clearly and distinctly stated how the blessed spirit of the seer opens itself to the Power in order to draw from its records and collections for the past, present and future, and to reproduce from them in words that which the Light allows to be given to mankind at the time of the fulfilments. –

In conclusion, let us once more be reminded that we, the pilgrims through the deep vale of the World of Matter, are not those at rest whom time passes by like landscapes at the window of a railway train, but *on the contrary those who are in motion.*

The way through the World of Matter of Subsequent Creation was not granted to us so that we should cling to earthly things and make them our idols, but for the sake of recognition. On this journey we are meant to grow and mature in spirit, so that this can one day leave the dense sphere of the World of

Matter in order to hasten fully conscious in the Ray of the Luminous Power towards the Spiritual Realm, where space and time eternally form a complete whole in the Living Power of the Creator.

GARDEN GNOMES

If our eyes were suddenly opened to enable us to see into the inner working of Nature, we should be lost in amazement and wonder.

Everywhere we should discover the forces active in Nature to be living beings, who take part eagerly and conscientiously in the coming into being and passing away in the vast realms of Nature.

All these small and great nature-beings, whom we may also call the small and great animistic beings*, have human forms, because, apart from their animistic core as basic species, they have within them a little of that which man bears within him as the core: the spiritual, which stipulates the human form.

If we could look more closely, we should also finally discover the original of the garden gnome of which approximate images, more or less well produced, adorn many gardens.

This glimpse behind the curtain of the beyond is of course possible only for such human beings as have the gift for it, thus who are clairvoyant. It is they who at some time or other have drawn the figures of the dwarfs or gnomes, and passed them on.

The little nature-beings, to whom the elves, as well as the nixies, salamanders, sylphs and so on belong, had already been active on earth long before man set foot on it for the first time. Without their participation there would be no mountains, meadows, rivers, lakes and seas.

---

* You can read about the great animistic beings, also called "gods" and "goddesses", in the essay "The Virtues" in the paperback: "Knowledge for the World of Tomorrow!"

The whole of Nature is animated by these faithful servants of God, who carry out His Will and Commandments most accurately in all things.

Since they swing selflessly in the Will of God they can neither be malicious nor do wrong. Only men have imputed such things to them.

All over the earth, from ancient and also more recent times, there are many traditions about the nature-beings. They are mentioned in the Bible, for example in the Gospel of Mark (4, 35–41), where it says: "And Jesus arose, and rebuked the wind, and said unto the sea, Peace, be still. And the wind ceased, and there was a great calm."

This simple, Biblical description expresses nothing other than that Jesus spoke to those nature-beings who are active in the elements of air and water.

Of Paracelsus, the famous physician and student of Nature in the Middle Ages, tradition has it that even as a boy he was able to see the little nature-beings at work in the lead mine at Kärnten. His father attended the miners there as a doctor.

The gnomes shared with him much knowledge of their activity, explaining the mysterious forces in flowers, metals and minerals, and how they were to be used for health and for the healing of illnesses. Later Paracelsus published a pamphlet on his experience with the water, earth, fire and air beings.

The people of former times saw and heard these beings much more than is the case today. It was a blessed working together, a joyful giving and receiving in helping and supporting love.

But for a long time now, with a few exceptions, men have through their ever-increasing materialistic attitude lost the connection with the helpers in the beyond. They were finally banished by them to the realm of fairy tales and fables.

Their real forms were rendered ever less true to nature, and the already-existing knowledge of their activity became superficial and merged in fantastic stories, which hardly correspond any longer to reality.

Last but not least, during certain times the knowledge of the nature-beings was forcibly suppressed as heresy.

Nevertheless the nature-beings still exist even today, in full activity. They direct and guide, tend and protect, foster and nourish, form and unite. On the astral plane they create wonderful prototypes and models for the gross matter of this earth.

Or they take part in the great flights of migratory birds, which contain so much that is mysterious to men, in which sun, stars and magnetic fields are indeed outwardly important; but behind it stand the animistic servants, controlling and helping.

They warn also of coming natural events, to which warnings animals are particularly sensitive. This, however, has nothing to do with either instinct or the sixth sense, but the animals simply see the nature-beings and recognise their warnings, because owing to their related species they are more receptive to them than men.

Animals then pass on the warnings to men through conspicuous behaviour, by which the lives of many have already been saved in this way.

In the Book of Numbers (22, 21–35) such a vision is described very expressively. The ass on which the Prophet Balaam was riding suddenly saw before it a higher being, an angel of the Lord holding a naked sword in his hand, and refused to go any further.

At first Balaam did not see the angel and struck the resisting ass three times, until his eyes were opened. Then he could also see the angel, and recognise that he himself was on the point of doing something wrong.

In their activity the nature-beings work with rays, which they bind, combine, lead towards and direct away from, and which so to speak are their instruments. Thus the little master-builders are also active in the coming into being of matter from atoms.

It will be a blessed and peaceful time when men are again able to take up the connection with the small and great beings of Nature. Clairvoyance is not absolutely necessary for this. It is enough if the human spirits through constant, genuine effort awaken in themselves the faculty of divining, and in their *inner perception* try to draw near to these beings.

Trust and a pure heart are what is needed for this. He who only wants to satisfy his curiosity or stimulate his imagination will find no connection.

But the servants of God still mourn over the human spirits who know everything better, whose arrogance and derision have already had to become silent in connection with many other intangible things, when that which previously could not be seen was in the meantime suddenly made visible through instruments that had been refined.

Certainly there are still people today who are able to see the nature-beings. But for the most part they remain silent about it, and keep their experiences to themselves, unless for once they meet people who are open for it, to whom their knowledge is of spiritual benefit. –

According to these explanations it is surely not so far-fetched to regard the "garden gnomes" as the symbol of the actually-existing little nature-beings, who also help human beings in manifold ways. But should the plaster gnomes be an inducement to concern ourselves more closely with the lovable living beings, then even they would fulfil a task not hitherto intended for them.

For it is remarkable how the use of these artificial garden gnomes has become so widespread in many countries. Perhaps this is also an indication of the fact that the beings of Nature are still quite strongly anchored in popular belief. But with an earnest volition, out of belief can one day grow again a knowledge of the realm of Nature in its full vitality.

For Nature is nothing other than the natural unfolding of the activity of the animistic servants. But for man Nature with all its animistic working is an indispensable step in his spiritual development on earth. The more he is linked with Nature, the sooner is he able to begin his spiritual ascent.

THE DISEASE OF CANCER

This terrible disease is rightly referred to as the "scourge of humanity". It is becoming ever more widespread, and up to the present time it still has not been possible to bring it under control.

Millions of people are stricken with it. Tens of thousands of scientists and medical men are striving to discover the cause of this disease. Millions are spent on cancer research every year. Experiments are constantly carried out in laboratories in order to find a solution.

However many cancer-agents there are, surely all must have something in common, which allows the healthy cell to become a cancerous cell.

Therefore the *fundamental* process must be sought. In doing so, we must include those beyond-earthly spheres which we are in a position to grasp only with the inner perception of our spirit.

First of all let us consider the cells of which the human body is composed.

At the beginning of the embryonic development there are no differing cells. Only during the development of the growing child's body do the cells differentiate from one another and form the individual organs of the body.

Now how do the cells come to unite into different organs? What forces regulate them in such a way that out of them are formed, for instance, the heart, the brain, the liver, the lymphatic system? Who provides the information for this?

Forces of nature that have taken on form, which we can also call nature-beings, are at work here. On the astral plane, which lies nearest to the World of Gross Matter, to the earthly, they create the astral body as a model, as a prototype, after which the child's body is only *subsequently* formed.

In this astral body, which is of finer matter, the whole design of the body, after which the corresponding cells then unite into organs and so on, must therefore be pre-formed or "programmed" by way of radiation. The astral body or the astral cloak is an important connecting-link between spirit, soul and body during the whole of earth-life. With physical death it disintegrates.

There is a good indication of the existence of the astral body: the *phantom-pains* which occur in a limb that no longer exists!

Why? Because the astral body, which has the form of the physical body, is not damaged when a limb is severed. It retains the limb severed from the physical body! Hence the pains in the missing physical limb, which really make themselves felt on the still existing astral limb, hitherto described as phantom because it is not visible to the physical eye. Phantom-pains cannot be without foundation but must have a body, where *they* can be *locally* felt.

Until now the often unbearable phantom-pains could mostly be treated only for a limited time with pain-killing drugs. But of late good results are being achieved with acupuncture, originating in China, which is applied to sound limbs. Through this phantom-pains can often be absent for months.

But let us return to the cells. It has been stated earlier that the whole physical structure is pre-formed by the nature-beings on the astral plane. This also includes the building-stones of the individual organs, the body cells with all their components.

Many of these components have been investigated by science.

These include for instance the nucleus, and the protoplasm surrounding the nucleus. In the nucleus are to be found the chromosomes, in which the genetic information or "heritage" is stored. All processes in the cell, which include above all the important cellular respiration, are regulated from within the nucleus.

Now there are yet other components of the cell, which are not visible to the physical eye. To these belong for instance minute spirit-particles, which stream from spiritual power-centres lying far above the Paradise of men right down to us, into the World of Gross Matter, where they give rise to the formation of elementary particles and atoms.

They are of course also to be found in the cell molecules, which are composed of atoms, and they have contact with the spiritual radiation of the human spirit incarnated in the physical body. For this reason they deserve special attention in the investigation into the cause of cancer.

Today the radiation of the human spirit is greatly weakened and dimmed through the predominantly materialistic attitude of earthmen, which is directed to this world. Therefore the radiation is hardly able any longer to exert an animating influence on the functions of the cells and organs, in order to achieve a "radiant health".

If we now imagine that to this generally weakened spiritual radiation there is further added a physical damage caused by long-lasting irritation of cells through toxins, then the structure of the cell molecules will be so altered that the regulation of the cells is greatly impeded. They can no longer receive the right information. This results in faulty regulation, and the oxygen supply gradually fails. As a consequence the cells begin to ferment, and together with substances of the nutrient fluid form an unrestrainedly increasing growth: the *cancerous tumour* as the *final* stage of a prolonged spiritual and physical disturbance.

The degeneration and unbridled growth of the affected cells also permeates even the surrounding healthy parts of the body. At the same time there is in addition the danger of parts of the cancer reaching distant areas of the body with the lymphatic or bloodstream, and giving rise to similar cancerous formations (metastases) there.

But the prolonged irritation of the cells through toxins calls for reference to one physical organ which should be given special attention in the investigation of cancer: *the liver!*

It is a miraculous work in itself. Its task is so many-sided that it can be described as an extraordinary organ. Apart from its activity as the most important detoxification-centre, it helps in multifarious ways with metabolism, among other things.

Therefore its disorder always affects the *whole* body profoundly. On the other hand the liver is capable of regenerating its own damaged cells, and even of rebuilding missing cells.

With normal activity everything is carefully converted, sifted and filtered in the liver. In the course of this toxins are broken down, made harmless and secreted. Hence the liver needs a constant good blood circulation. A healthy liver ensures pure blood.

If, however, it becomes diseased, it is no longer in a position to break down the various toxins sufficiently; these will penetrate into the circulation, causing chronic conditions of irritation in the cell-tissue, and so create the soil for cancer.

Consequently with preventive measures and with cancerous diseases the toxins forming in the body in the process of metabolism, and the toxic substances entering it from outside must not be overlooked, in connection with which above all the kind of nutrition and the metabolism play an important part, the more so if through heredity there is already a tendency towards cancer. But also environmental factors which have a direct cancer-evoking influence from outside on the cells, as for example chemical substances and foreign rays (X-rays, radio-activity, earth-rays), have to be taken into account.

According to present-day knowledge the resistance-potential of the body cells to cancer is limited. Therefore efforts are being made to discover ways and means of stimulating the body to render cancer harmless, rather than nourishing it.

But here again it should be remembered that the liver is the most important organ in *cancer-resistance!*

Already in 1929 Abd-ru-shin, Author of The Grail Message, *"In the Light of Truth"*, wrote in the journal *"Der Ruf"* *("The Call")*, publication for all progressive knowledge, number 13, under the "Medical Section", Cancer Research:

"Any cancerous growth is conditioned by the incapacity and insufficient activity of the liver! This must be borne in mind. A healthy liver with a really normal activity does not permit any kind of cancer to develop. Therefore among young people a correspondingly sensible way of living should already be strictly observed. Even among those already ill, the emphasis should be placed mainly on that! With the recovery of the liver the power of the illness is broken, no matter where it is located."

This text was again published in 1953 in the book *"Fragen-beantwortungen"* (The Grail Message Foundation Publishing Co. – English edition: *"Questions and Answers"*, 1972). In a lecture given by Abd-ru-shin in 1935, which was published in German in 1950 and in English in 1959 (Vol. III of The Grail Message, *The Destroyed Bridge)* he mentions once again the importance of the liver:

"Quite apart from the smokers themselves, having to breathe

in such tobacco smoke hampers the normal development of many an organ in infants and children, especially the necessary firmness and strengthening of the liver, which is particularly important for every person, because when functioning in the *right* and healthy manner it can prevent the establishment of a cancerous centre as the surest and best means of resistance to this plague."

Meantime this recognition has spread further. Thus *Dr. A. Vogel*, Teuffen, Switzerland, writes in his book *"The Little Doctor"* (1973 Edition, published privately):

"The liver is the most important barrier in the fight against cancer. As long as this miraculous laboratory is functioning well, a cancerous degeneration of the cells cannot take place. Since the liver thereby occupies a key position in the fight against cancer, we should seek to maintain it for ourselves as an efficient barrier because, as has been stated before, cancer will then be given no opportunity to develop."

In his book *"The Liver as Regulator of Health"* (1975, *A. Vogel*, Teuffen, Switzerland), *Dr. Vogel* mentions the following in the chapter on *"Cancer and the Liver"*:

"On one of my trips to America I had a discussion with one of the best-known cancer researchers, who on the basis of his many years of experience confirmed to me that no cancer patient had yet been brought to his clinic who did not have a disturbed functioning of the liver and pancreas. Since other cancer researchers have also expressed similar views about these connections, it can in fact be said: no cancer without a malfunctioning of the liver and pancreas."

Dr. H. Anemueller, in his book *"Health through Sensible Nutrition and Diet"* (1963, Paracelsus Publishing Co.), explains:

"It should be borne in mind that in every case of cancer the liver is damaged, and its performance greatly impaired. For this reason alone the food-intake must be limited. The restoration of a normal liver function is one of the most important objectives of the dietetic treatment of cancer."

The English researcher *Caspar Blond*, M.D., wrote in the medical journal *"Hippocrates"* (Vol. 11, 1956) to this effect:

"Cancer is the result of a chronically progressive liver-insufficiency. There is no doubt that food poisons play a part in this."

(Liver-insufficiency means an inadequate working capacity of the liver.)

The importance of the liver is also shown by its significance in the interrelations between spirit, soul and body. It is more subject than other digestive glands to the influence of the frame of mind. Not for nothing are there such (German) popular sayings as: "A louse has run over his liver", when someone is irritable or annoyed, or "anger gnawed at his liver", thus damaging his health. And one who is extremely irate "spews venom and bile", which is produced by the liver. Even the Babylonians had a greeting: "May your liver become smooth!" This meant: "Do not be angry, moderate your anger."

The word hypochondriac (a sufferer from morbid depression) is related to "hypochondrium", by which is meant the area under the arch of the ribs, thus in the region of the liver, which points to the fact that this disease is associated with the liver.

Not for nothing has the word *liver* an identity of sound with *life!*

But the majority of men have more and more distanced themselves from real life and thus also from Nature. Man is no longer linked with Nature!

Therefore he must again become alive in spirit, and a

necessary step towards this is *Nature!* Liberation from the hitherto-existing unnatural way of life lies in observing the Laws of Nature. –

But man should give more consideration to his physical body right from the earliest years, and not only when pain makes itself felt. He should earn the foundation for a natural way of living in future, and above all practise a *wise moderation.* This refers for example to *right nutrition, breathing, movement, personal hygiene and balance between work and rest.* For after all the physical body is the most important instrument which the Creator has entrusted to us for our *spiritual* development, the goal of which is not the earth, but the Paradise of the human spirits that lies far above it.

But more than anything man must not forget Nature when he is ill, and must remember the old Biblical word which still applies today: "God hath created medicines out of the earth, And let not a discerning man reject them" (Sirach 38, 4). The whole of Nature, with its manifold healing powers, gives him the best helps and remedies for health and disease – even for the disease of cancer.

However, the remedies alone are not enough. In all illnesses it is necessary for the spirit of man himself to *help with* his recovery, in order to ensure a permanent cure. If he merely lets the remedies do their work, the recovery will not last long, since the cause of it has not been removed. In the final analysis the cause lies with the human spirit, with its *free will,* with which he *himself creates* his environment as well as *his diseases,* regardless of whether this happens only in this earth-life, or whether dim threads of fate from earlier lives cause diseases hidden in his physical heritage to manifest.

But just as man creates the diseases for himself, so is he likewise in a position to do away with them by giving up his materialistic attitude, and humbly directing his gaze upwards, to Luminous Heights.

Only from thence come strengthening radiations which allow his spirit to glow. In its once more pure and powerful radiation his sick body can then recover its health, supported by the healing gifts of Nature.

But if it is already too late for an effective cure, it is a comfort and a help to know that *only the earthly cloak* can be diseased, never the spirit, which with its finer coverings forms the soul.

Also the sick person can so purify his spirit that at his earthly death, freed from the burden of the diseased physical body, he may joyfully rise upwards into those Blessed Fields which, far from earthly pain and earthly suffering, exist in the Light of Divine Grace!

THE BLOOD AS IDENTITY CARD

At the beginning of the 20th century the four blood groups A, B, AB and 0 were discovered. Since then many details concerning the blood and its composition have become known to science. These include also the discovery of further blood group systems, and the establishing of blood formulas for racial groups, families and individuals.

According to the most recent research, connections are also revealed between blood groups and diseases. Thus one group is less susceptible to certain diseases than another. In plagues the one blood group is likewise less at risk, while it is harder for the other group to overcome them.

Scientists are said to be even now certain that with further refinement of the differences they will be in a position in the foreseeable future to determine a personal blood formula for every human being, so that one day there will hardly be two persons whose formulas correspond in every detail.

This has led to the observation that the individual composition of a person's blood is comparable to an identity card, because this is clearly adjusted to the person of the holder.

The assumption that every human being must have his own blood formula, which reflects only his particular nature, is right.

It is based on a process that has hitherto remained unrecognised, and which was made known only by Abd-ru-shin in his Grail Message, in the lecture "The Mystery of the Blood".

With his explanation, *"the spirit forms the human blood"*, he gave a completely new, fundamental recognition.

Why it is the spirit that forms the blood is shown by the

fact that the blood exists only while the spirit is present in the body. Only with the entry of the spirit into the developing child's body about the middle of pregnancy does the blood form in the small body and begin to circulate.

When the spirit leaves the body at earthly death, thus when earthman "gives up the ghost", the blood is no longer there either. The arteries are empty of blood. The blood has lost its form, and only congealed residues of blood are still in the veins.

Now since every spirit – with its finer coverings called soul – has its *free will* from its origin, the spiritual development is different with each human being. No two persons are alike in this. Every human being develops and uses his abilities and qualities in a way differing from that of his fellow-man. Therefore to place men on the same level and make them equal is contrary to the Laws of Creation.

Hence every spirit also forms its blood in a different composition, in the way peculiar to itself, so that if an exact analysis should one day be possible, the personal blood formulas will never be identical, just as in the case of finger-prints.

Therefore it is understandable that at all times more has been suspected in the blood than only the fulfilment of physical functions. There was always a divining of the interrelations between spirit and blood, and many sayings and expressions indicate how closely connected the blood is with the spirit.

Thus, for example, for something to "pass into one's flesh and blood" (German) means to have assured mastery of something, to absorb something completely, it becomes second nature, as it were. This includes not only comprehending with the "fleshly" brain, but also grasping with the spirit, which is figuratively indicated by the blood.

The reaction of spiritual expressions instantly affects the

blood, when it drains from the face with agitation, when horror makes it curdle, when someone turns crimson with shame, or when a person's "blood runs cold", thus when he is very afraid.

All these confirm the recognition that the spirit forms the blood.

The further investigation of the blood and the knowledge of its real purpose have undreamed-of consequences for a future healthy development of the human spirit on earth.

MECHANISMS OF EVIL

At all times there have been people who were able to see and read thoughts. But if thoughts can be seen, then they must represent something, and have content and form. However these forms are of finer matter than the coarse earthly. They can therefore be perceived only by those human beings whose inner eye is opened for it, thus who are clairvoyant.

Similarly the helpers in the beyond can read our thoughts, and make use of this possibility to help us, to give us advice and to appeal to our conscience. In special cases they can even employ the radiations of pure thought-channels, to work through these right into the coarse earthly.

One need not be clairvoyant, however, to be convinced of the reality of thoughts. There are still other indications of their existence: the transference of thoughts from one person to another without giving utterance to the thoughts. We read about it from time to time, or have experienced for ourselves how thoughts which we direct at a particular person, which are "intended" for him, are picked up by him, as it afterwards turned out. In this connection distance plays no part; just as little does the fact that the people may be inside houses at the time of these transferences. Thoughts are simply lighter and finer than gross matter, and therefore are able to penetrate walls in the same way as radio-waves.

For a long time now man has been in a position to measure thought-waves. Another proof that they have substance, the radiations of which can be determined by means of the finest instruments.

Real thoughts are glowed through by the inner perception of the spirit. Otherwise they are cold and feeble.

They arise through the activity of the frontal brain (large brain). From the thoughts in turn is formed intellect. As the brain belongs to the earthly, is part of the perishable body, it likewise ceases to exist at death. Accordingly it is no longer possible for man to think and to use his intellect in the beyond. In their place appear other means of communication.

For this reason the intellect is only able to grasp earthly things. Anything that goes beyond this is no longer "understood" by it. One is simply at one's wits' end, the understanding comes to an end, or it is beyond the intellect, as soon as it is a question of extra-sensory, extra-earthly things, which come into the sphere of spiritual comprehension only.

However perishable the brain, the thoughts generated by it nevertheless continue to exist because, as they are formed, radiations of a finer nature are received, which permit the thoughts to outlive the death of the gross material body.

In this way they also belong to the works which follow man at his death (Revelation 14, 13). In the beyond they await the departed soul, and hold it fast in gloomy lowlands if the thoughts were of an evil nature, or in the case of good thoughts they form a path for a gladdening progress into lighter regions.

In his book "Heavenly Thoughts" Karl May, who knew or divined more than his narratives allow one to realise, says on this subject: "Every man is the creator of his own world. His deeds are the solid, his words the fluid, his thoughts the imponderable (weightless) components of this world. He not only makes it for himself for here, but will not be able to renounce it in that life either."

Recently thoughts and their transference (telepathy) have become the subject of exhaustive scientific research. But as is usual today, the results are mostly not used for constructive purposes.

So, for example, people are eagerly exploring the extent to which telepathy as so-called mental radio would be practicable in wars, in espionage, in politics; and they are already considering how the thoughts of enemies in war can be confused, and how it may be possible for thought-transference to be prevented or distorted through jamming-stations.

But this is not yet enough. The abuse goes further. Through the concentrated influence on human brains, they wish forcibly to exercise a total thought-power on larger groups of people.

It is not possible, however, to break down a person's moral barrier through the evil volition of others, nor even through telepathic encroachments upon his private life, against the will of the person concerned. With firm confidence in spiritual help anyone can summon enough will-power to ward off evil thoughts, and not allow them to take effect in his personal sphere.

Of what use is all this research if people neglect above all to learn details about the nature and effect of thoughts, with a view to a spiritual upward striving and to a healthy earthly upbuilding.

We can no longer remain indifferent spectators of a happening which each day brings new, evil surprises, but are now forced to concern ourselves seriously with problems which lie outside our sensory perceptions, that is to say, in the spiritual sphere, because ultimately our *spiritual survival* also depends on it.

The view was recently expressed that crimes could possibly be prevented if, through basic research, adequate information were obtained about the mechanisms which at regular intervals drive human beings to the collective crime of genocide.

These mechanisms, or rather collective actions, are rooted in part in the dark thought-centres, of which there are as many as the crimes man is able to devise. But there are also thought-centres of peace and pure love.

In accordance with the Law of the Attraction of Homogeneous Species, similar thoughts unite in centres. These in turn are connected with homogeneous spheres of Darkness and of Light.

All those involved in them are linked with these concentrations of evil or of good by threads, and receive via this line of connection an ever new supply, which allows evil as well as good to grow within them. And some day the moment comes when one or several persons, or whole masses, will transform for example an evil which at first was embodied only in thought-forms, into deeds somewhere on earth, and in this way perpetrate a *collective crime*. There are no earthly barriers in this. All of them, in whatever country they may be, are connected with one another through a *real collective guilt*.

Thus it happens that we hear of crimes of a similar nature perpetrated in the most diverse parts of the earth. "It is in the air", as the popular saying goes. Something unpleasant or disastrous is impending. But to this "air" also belong the thought-forms with their radiations, which press towards realisation, and wherever there are weak or dark places the fruits of evil volition manifest on earth.

Such cases are now brought to our attention nearly every day. Let us for instance only consider the new types of crimes. First there is a "precedent", an isolated case, which then as a chain reaction is followed by others.

Of the "thought-sinners" only the wrongdoers whose deeds are physically visible can be caught and convicted. The remaining "accomplices" stay at large because their complicity is invisible.

All, however, *without exception,* are subject to the Laws of

Creation, which in their incorruptibility provide for a just reaction; but also for the severance of the dark threads of fate, if the readiness for it exists in the originator through a continuing good volition and conduct.

In contrast to the foregoing statements, a collective crime pictured according to earthly interpretation, which places the burden of the criminal deeds of individual members on the community (nation, family), cannot be substantiated either legally or morally.

For on earth, where the homogeneous species are not separated, participants and non-participants, the guilty and the innocent, find themselves intermingled in a community.

If therefore a collective guilt is thrown upon a community, those not involved are also implicated and morally degraded (discriminated against).

From all the explanations it is already evident that thoughts *cannot be free*. On the contrary, we must often pay even a very heavy penalty for them. In ancient times there was a saying: "No one is punished for his thoughts." Later this was changed to the proverb: "Thoughts are free."

If a man allows bad thoughts to arise within him, they are not free, thus not free from punishment. According to the simple Law, "What a man sows he must reap", these thoughts return many times over to their originator as evil fate, which was put into the world by himself. Man has at all times full responsibility for what he thinks and does.

How important it is then also *to be alert in thought,* and to examine what "goes through one's head". Above all, reflection on the world of thoughts should increasingly prompt us to awaken and cultivate within us the concept of the pure and noble, so that we shall not one day have to reproach ourselves with being involved through frivolous thoughts in the evil

deeds of others, which deep in our hearts we detest and condemn.

If we bestow as much purity as possible on our thoughts, we thereby further the thought-centres of good, and help to eliminate the "thought-garbage" that devastatingly contributes to the environmental pollution in the beyond and on this side, and thus gradually to close down the "mechanisms of evil" to which the dark thought-centres also belong. They must then wither and dry up, because they no longer receive any supply. Therein also lies ultimately the prevention of all crime.

THE GRACE OF GOD

Although the Law of Reciprocal Action (Seed and Harvest) is strict and inexorable like all the Laws in Creation, yet the Grace of God has also been woven into it. Only this gives man the *possibility at all* of being able to redeem a transgression against a Divine Law or Commandment, thus an offence, a sin, as soon as he has recognised his wrong volition in the experiencing, and in steadfast striving turns inwardly to the good. That is a Grace of God which many people endeavour in vain to understand, perhaps also because they think that they must deny the re-embodiments of the human spirit which in many cases are necessary for redemption, thus deny the possibility of repeated earth-lives granted to the human spirits by God.

And yet this Grace of God – in contrast to the Luciferian principle of merciless temptation and seduction of the human spirits to sin – is unutterably vast and great to human understanding. Without this Grace of redemption, man would never be in a position to free himself from the burden of his sins. He would have to carry it around with him eternally.

The question of whether Divine Grace is given unconditionally, or whether it is dependent on the fulfilment of the Divine Commandments, is answered by the Law of Balance between giving and receiving, to which Jesus referred with His words, "It is more blessed to give than to receive" (Acts 20, 35).

Something must be given by the human spirit as balance, as counter-value for the Grace: *trust in God* and His Will, which is closely bound up *with the observance of His Laws and Commandments*. Trust is the basis for the help of God, for His "Forgiving Grace".

The concept of Grace must therefore not be taken *one-sidedly*. Forgiveness is not possible through faith alone, if faith is not followed by the good deed.

Thus man also experiences the extraordinary Grace of God in the *pre-redemption* of his evil karma, if he honestly strives to give purity to his inner perceptions and thoughts, and to adjust his doing and thinking to the Laws of Creation. In time he thereby creates for himself an increasingly pure ethereal environment, which must eventually have a definite effect on all that is earthly.

He gradually loosens his dark fetters, imbues his surroundings with refreshing, upbuilding spiritual currents, thereby effecting the mitigation or disintegration of returning karmaically-stipulated dark currents by the lighter radiation. Finally the redemption continues to take place only symbolically, in which "chance" may "play a part" through strange guidance and Providence; or situations arise of which we might perhaps say that it could have had a worse ending. With that a feeling of inner relief spreads, as though something menacing, something dangerous had brushed against or passed by us.

With this also we experience one of the many manifestations of Grace which the Creator has bestowed upon us in His Laws.

It is a further Grace that the human spirit is permitted to dwell in this wonderful Creation, in order with a free volition to mature in it to a fully conscious personality. This can take place in complete harmony and joy. For sorrow and pain are not necessary for it. These are brought in by man alone. They are not willed by God!

How often we beg that God's great Grace may be upon us. But have we even once considered *wherein* God's Grace lies?

THE ETERNAL COUNSEL OF GOD

Anything that befalls man in the way of hardship is very often called fate, and looked upon as a higher power which determines his life.

But in reality it is men themselves who shape their fate or karma, which depending on their free decisions is either good or bad, exactly in accordance with the Law that he who has sown it must reap the seed many times over, even if it be only in later earth-lives. Every moment man gives cause for fateful consequences in the future, and every moment he stands in the reactions of previous decisions from the present and from past earth-lives.

Thus men living on earth today must also be answerable to themselves for what they willed and thought in former earth-lives. In this connection it matters not whether the volition was general or directed at definite other human beings. This should exhort us to act with caution, and heighten our sense of responsibility, so that in the future, whether on earth or in the beyond, evil reactions that darken and make our lives painful will no longer be possible.

Therefore let everyone who is struck by more or less severe "blows of fate" remember above all that *he* is the originator, and not some other person.

Perhaps at one time he has done something evil to a fellow human being, who had to suffer from it *innocently*. To the innocent sufferer the Laws of Creation always bring a compensation in some form or other, provided he forgives the wrongdoer. But to the guilty one dark threads of karma become attached at the very moment of the deed, which unfailingly return to him as the fruits of his volition. This is then the

"punishment" which he inflicts upon himself. In reality it is the just balance of his evil volition, the real "compulsion to atonement".

From this point of view the doctrine of *predestination* must be considered differently from hitherto. According to this it is believed that the decree of God, firmly-established from eternity, determines who among men is admitted to eternal bliss and who is doomed to eternal damnation. This gives the impression that *from the outset* a definite number of human beings are allowed to attain to eternal salvation, and another definite number are eternally lost.

Against this stands the free will of decision bestowed on men by God, which implies that it lies solely with man himself whether he wishes to strive upwards or downwards. The executors of his decisions are then the Laws of Creation which, in carrying out his free will, let him attain to Luminous Heights or to dark depths.

What *Karl May* says in his book "Heavenly Thoughts" points also in this direction:

"Do not smile about it, for it is true: Your thoughts, words and works are recorded in the 'Book of Life' by none other than yourself."

Thus the decision for eternal life or for eternal death lies not with God but only with man. He himself bears the responsibility for his deeds and thoughts, which lead him upwards or downwards. Through His Laws God only allows the decisions of men to be carried out.

Only in this is revealed to human beings the *Eternal Counsel of God* (Psalm 33, 11), which from the inception of Creation is expressed in His immutable Laws, and which is closely linked with the *Omniscience of God* that cannot be separated from Justice and Love.

THE TRUMPETS OF THE WORLD JUDGMENT

Through the Fall of Man, through the turning away from God, humanity have contributed much, very much, to intensifying *for themselves* the World Judgment, which is now heading towards its climax.

Not without reason is a *suicidal programme* by mankind being spoken and written about today, a sinister, gruesome programme, the obstinate execution of which brings ominously near the danger of total self-destruction.

In this programme the earth plays a special role. Exploited, devastated and besmirched through wanton deeds and thoughts, it moves through space; the earth, once made over to men to hold in trust for their responsible use and spiritual maturing, as a starting-point from which, as on a heavenly ladder, they could have entered directly into Paradise.

The forces of Nature bestowed treasures and fruits of this earth in full measure on the individual peoples, to make natural use of and to heed them as a protection and support for their spiritual progress.

But they were meant and indeed had to pass on their surplus, in strict obedience to the Law of Balance between giving and receiving.

However the gifts of Nature, which through a stimulating and invigorating exchange should have contributed to peace and harmonious working, are very often unscrupulously misused to the injury, suppression and destruction of fellow human beings.

The great comprehensive Law of Creation, to maintain always a just balance in giving as well as in receiving, in every respect and in all spheres of life, has already for a long time simply been heeded no more.

Is it not then an inevitable consequence that through the guilt of men the world is falling to pieces, plunging out of balance, which now in the World Judgment must be forcibly restored through the Will of God?

There are many signs by which men on earth can recognise this unique World Judgment.

Certainly they ponder over these, but they apply to every event only the yardstick of their intellect, and not that of their inner perception. In so doing, however, they never measure themselves! Now they must experience that their keenest intellectual acumen cannot make up for the emptiness of their souls, and that striving only for earthly things must not be regarded as the highest goal.

There is no continuing development for man in this, because the spirit within him urges towards higher things. He must *awaken* the noble abilities slumbering within him, so that he is able consciously to fulfil his task in Creation: to be a connecting link between the World of Matter and his homeland, the Spiritual Realm, in that already down here and later from above he has a furthering, upbuilding and ennobling influence upon this world. Therein lies the *meaning of life,* which is also decisive for the future Kingdom of Peace.

A Kingdom of Peace that is founded by the Divine Will requires human beings who have recognised the meaning of life. Only they are able to bear within them and to spread abroad true peace.

But where are such human beings to be found today and what must yet come to pass in terms of suffering before they are ripe for the new Kingdom of Peace that is to be established on earth after the World Judgment!

As yet the earth is still heavily weighed down by the oppressive burden which mankind have forced upon it over thousands of years through their evil deeds and volition.

Indeed how very tiny is this earth in the enormous expanses of the Universe, and how great the Grace of God which is granted to it at this Turning-Point. For it is chosen to be a point of anchorage for the Radiations of the Light.

Soon there will also glow for it in the end-time of the World Judgment the dawn of a future in purity and beauty, with a humanity who have humbly and gratefully recognised the Will of their Lord and God, and who live in accordance with It.

Before this, however, humanity must patiently endure the purifying waves of the World Judgment in order to wash their souls clean in them and to become new in themselves.

Many indeed know of the coming of this World Judgment but they are still awaiting the *trumpet-blasts* which are to herald it.

Let those who thus wait follow attentively just for once the news from the countries of the earth. Each day brings reports of political disturbances, economic distress, famine, of outrages and dreadful misery; plagues and drought afflict mankind, the earth quakes and destroys whole cities within seconds, deadly hurricanes rage along, volcanoes belch forth devastating fire, rivers overflow their banks, tearing away homesteads, cattle and men.

Are these not trumpet-blasts for the Judgment, when here today and there tomorrow the waves of terror and dread roll over mankind, to shake them violently awake even at the last moment? What is sinister and new in this is the abundance of events never before experienced, the speed with which they follow one another.

But who allows himself to be touched by them, unless they directly affect him personally?

And yet even as one "not actually involved" he could in certain circumstances greatly mitigate his burden of fate, which will one day also strike him in the World Judgment.

For if he does not close himself to other people's distress and suffering, and exerts himself to experience and inwardly perceive it with them, then something begins to flower within him which will envelop him like a protective mantle: *compassion*, which selflessly seeks to help all human beings who still bear within them a spark of longing for the Light!

In the midst of all the confusion he will then receive the help of God in the same measure as he opens himself to the Light, and will thus be able to give comfort and confident hope to many wounded souls!

"WHICH IS TO COME" (Rev. 1,4)

At the beginning of his Revelation John conveys Grace "from him, which is, and which was, and *which is to come ... and* from Jesus Christ". These are quite obviously *two* Persons Who are spoken of. "Which is to come" *and* Jesus!

God Himself will not descend into Creation, because it would have to perish in the enormous Power of His Divinity. But He can sever a Part of Himself and send It into Creation, as happened with Jesus. In exactly the same way God severed yet another Part of Himself, the Son of Man, Whom Jesus promised at the time of His earthly existence and Whose Name Isaiah proclaimed in his prophecy: Imanuel! (Matthew 25, 31; Isaiah 7, 14).

He is the Creator and Upholder of the whole of Creation, He is the Word through Which all things are made, and of Whom it was proclaimed: "In the beginning was the Word, and the Word was with God, and the Word was God" (John 1, 1). It was *He* to Whom John referred when he spoke of Him Which is to come: Imanuel, the Son of Man!

The entire Creation came into being in the Radiation of the Son of Man. And with it also the human spirits. Later, in Subsequent Creation (the World of Matter), many of them of their own volition pursued wrong courses, withdrawing ever further from God. To free them from their confusion and entanglement – for they themselves were no longer able to do so – God in His great Love severed from Himself a second Part, and allowed It to "become flesh": Jesus of Nazareth.

The Son of Man could not yet come at that time because He was being prepared for His Mission ordained for a later period. But mankind, who had become engulfed in Darkness, needed immediate help. It was a Divine Act of Emergency, and when Jesus saw how little His Word was heeded and observed, or in Biblical words, when He perceived that "the darkness comprehended him not" (John 1, 5), He promised the coming of the Son of Man, Who "would guide them into all truth" (John 16, 13).

Thus in the Divine Kingdom Imanuel is the First-born and Jesus the Second-born Son of God. But in the World of Matter, on earth, Jesus was "the first begotten of the dead" (Revelation 1, 5), for He incarnated there first in order to help men, who were as though dead spiritually, whereas Imanuel followed Him only later, as the Judge appointed by God in the Final Judgment.

His judicial activity is described exactly in the Revelation. Through John He sends His judgments to the seven World-Churches, also to our World-Church Ephesus, after closely examining them, for "all the churches shall know that I am he which searcheth the reins and hearts" (Revelation 2, 23). Here the rein, the organ of purification, stands for purity, and the heart for the inner perception of the spirit. The human spirit is searched as to how, in the course of his development, he has used his inner perception. What is decisive in the Judgment is the purity of his inner perceptions, thoughts and deeds.

All the dreadful ethereal forms of sin which men have put into the World through their wrong deeds and thoughts, including the great city of Babylon and the beasts, will be destroyed in the great Final Judgment through the Radiation-Power of the Son of Man.

He also vanquishes the "dragon" (Lucifer), chaining him for a thousand years, so that men can help undisturbed with the upbuilding of the Millennium on earth (Revelation 20, 1-3).

His Word is as a "sharp twoedged sword", by which the "nations" must judge themselves (Revelation 1, 16; 19, 15).

The concept for the word "nations" (Revelation 19, 15; 20, 3; 21, 24), like much else in the Revelation, must not be taken in the earthly sense. It is intended as a concept of Creation for those human spirits who are still in the development-stage in the Material World (Subsequent Creation) below Paradise, whereas the word "Jews" in the Revelation describes all those human spirits who have attained to a higher development and are already matured spiritually. Only thus is the utterance to be understood: "and I know the blasphemy of them which say they are Jews (that is, spiritually mature human beings), and are not" (Revelation 2, 9; 3, 9).

At the end of the Revelation the Son of Man says: "And, behold, I come quickly; and my reward is with me, to give every man according as his work shall be" (22, 12). Those words clearly indicate that man himself must receive the corresponding reward for his good and bad deeds. This is based on the personal responsibility of the human spirit, which he cannot throw upon anyone else, also not upon Jesus. "The Lamb of God, which beareth* the sin of the world" (John 1, 29), does not mean that Jesus has taken or will take away their sins from men. Such an easy taking-away of sins is opposed to all the Laws of Creation. On the contrary, it is meant to express that it can be seen from the wound-marks of Jesus what sin men have committed against Him in having "slain Him like a Lamb" without guilt (Revelation 5, 12).

Hence men cannot cast their sins upon Jesus (Isaiah 53, 6), but in virtue of their own responsibility they themselves must bear their burden of guilt; or, as we also read in the Revela-

---

* (Lutheran Bible)

94

tion: Men must themselves wash their robes (souls) and make them white (7, 14). Only the Word of God can help them in this. If they strive to observe It, their souls will become pure, and they will be able to pass in the Judgment.

But then they will also recognise the Son of Man proclaimed by Jesus, Who already had His being before the beginning of Creation. "I am Alpha and Omega, the beginning and the end, the first and the last," says the Son of Man of Himself (Revelation 22, 13). The beginning, because through Him Creation came into being, and the end, because He would remain as the Last if His Creation should ever cease to exist.

He is likewise the Spirit of God, Who is also called the "Holy Spirit". With the Words "Let there be light" (Genesis 1, 3) His Radiation surged across the boundary of the Divine Kingdom into the Universe that was void of Light, and from this Radiation there was formed in the beginning the First Creation, Primordial Creation. With this Happening the Holy Spirit did not become merged in His Creation. Hence in the account of Creation, which is to be understood spiritually, it is clearly stated: "And the Spirit of God moved *upon* the face of the waters (Creation)" (Genesis 1, 2).

To make it possible for Creation to remain in existence forever, and to prevent Imanuel from being drawn back by the mighty Radiation-Power of God, a small Part of Him was incarnated in Primordial Creation, and thus most closely linked with that kind of species in which humanity have their origin. Thus He became the Son sent by God to men, *the Son of Man,* the link from God to mankind, *the Eternal Mediator.*

But the Part put forth into Primordial Creation is "Parsifal", King of the Holy Grail, Who is in the Grail Castle, and linked with the Son of Man Imanuel in the Divine Kingdom by an unbreakable bond of radiation. These are two Personalities,

Imanuel – Parsifal, but they are one in their working. For example, in the Revelation the Angel who comes down from Heaven (20, 1-3) and binds the dragon (Lucifer) is synonymous with Parsifal.

Now it is also clear why the Son of Man Imanuel must be called the "Outborn Son", whereas Jesus, Who has again become one with the Father, is the Inborn Son. He is King in the Divine Kingdom, whereas Imanuel is King of the whole of Creation.

Most closely bound up with the Son of Man is the happening of the Sealing. 144,000 human spirits were "sealed in their foreheads" (Revelation 7, 3) in the Spiritual Realm. They were to bear on their foreheads the Sign of God, the equal-armed Cross, the Sign of the Truth, after vowing loyally to serve God and His two Sons, namely "Him which sitteth upon the throne" (Imanuel) and "the Lamb" (Jesus) (Revelation 7, 10), and to help the Son of Man in the upbuilding of the new Kingdom of God. An Act of Sealing on earth is based on the same vow.

The twelve tribes mentioned signify that those sealed were chosen from the twelve different groups of mankind. Each of these groups has a special homogeneity rooted in the spiritual talents and virtues (Revelation 7, 4-8).

As the Upbuilder of Creation, the Son of Man sustains and renews it. The Source of renewal and sustenance is the Holy Grail, the "fountain of the water of life" (Revelation 21, 6), which is in the Grail Castle, the "temple of God" (Revelation 11, 19; 15, 5).

The Grail, a Chalice, contains the Eternal Power which through the Son of Man is poured out into Creation once a year.

Man must gradually make himself familiar with the thought that not only on earth are all things formed, but also beyond the earth in the supra-earthly regions, though from finer, lighter species of Creation. Indeed the earth is only the coarsest image of the already existing supra-earthly prototypes, which are far more perfect and beautiful than the forms visible to us. Thus later on, in the new era of peace, there shall one day be built on earth an image of the supra-earthly Grail Castle.

This Grail Castle stands, in fact, at the highest place in Primordial Spiritual Creation, far above the Paradise of men. It is the only point of connection between God and His Creation; it could also be said that it is an intersection point of radiations, a transformation-centre for the Radiation-Power which comes from the Divine Kingdom above it, and is passed on through *the Son of Man, the Creative Will of God,* into the lower-lying Creation.

The human spirit, too, lives from this pure Power, but unfortunately has for the greater part applied it wrongly, and misused it for base purposes.

Just as the heart allows the blood to pulsate through the body, so the Spiritual Power streams out of the Grail through Creation at regular intervals. The pulse-beat of the heart is a reflection of this mighty pulse-beat of Eternal Life, because everything that takes place "above" is repeated "below", in many variations.

In the Revelation John describes many events relating to the Grail. His spiritual eye beheld mighty happenings, which he was allowed to mediate and pass on to mankind. In Jesus' day the time had not yet come for men to be able to grasp the Knowledge of the Grail, but now the stage has been reached in the development of mankind where the Knowledge of Creation also includes the Knowledge of the Grail.

This Knowledge will give the spiritual character to the new era which is now dawning with the Cosmic Turning-Point, because then the human spirit will be able consciously and gratefully to receive the spiritual Power, the Water of Life, streaming from out of the Grail, for the blessing and joy of all creatures in Creation.

Therefore the words at the end of the Revelation are full of promise: "And let him that is athirst come. And whosoever will, let him take the water of life freely" (22, 17). To him who uses this Power aright the Gate to Paradise will open, and he will be permitted to receive the crown of life (Revelation 2, 10), the gift of being allowed to live eternally.

Whereas at that time the words of John, who as John the Baptist on earth "bore record of the word of God, and of the testimony of Jesus Christ" (Revelation 1, 2) were: "Grace be unto you from him which is to come," it should today read: "Grace from Him Who has come." For meanwhile the great promise of the coming of a second Son of God into Creation has been fulfilled. As in those days Jesus, the Son of God, brought the Word, so today is it proclaimed by the Son of Man, Imanuel. For both are Sons of God, and one in God!

"BUT WHEN THE SON OF MAN COMETH..."

1.

The handing down of spoken words is a difficult problem, especially when spiritual values are to be conveyed. How easily gaps of memory occur in the course of transmission, and how much people are inclined to fill these gaps with ideas corresponding to their own way of thinking and their own views, so that the original meaning of what was said is often entirely lost.

Unfortunately the words of Jesus as recorded in the New Testament are no exception here, still less so since they were not collected and written down until decades after His physical death. The authors based their writings on oral transmission or written notes, with which they also interwove their own views.

As regards the sayings of Jesus, we are dealing not with intellectually-bound earthly explanations but with spiritual explanations and teachings which comprise the entire knowledge of Creation and which were partly misunderstood right from the beginning, and were then also passed on as such. For Jesus Himself said that in some things He had not been understood by His hearers, indeed not even by His disciples. In the very transmission of what was not understood, an alteration of what Jesus really said is inevitable.

Everyone knows that even after a short time he cannot exactly reproduce something he has heard, and if there were several listeners each one would describe it differently. This was already the same in past millennia, and even spiritual inspiration could never quite eliminate it in the case of the disciples and the authors of the Gospels, although their intentions were of the best.

That this problem of transmission also troubles theological circles, and not only at the present time, is shown in the explanations of D. Johannes Weiss, Professor of Divinity, in his essay, "The Three Older Gospels" (1907). In this he assumes that the Gospel of Mark was written approximately 40 years after Jesus' life on earth. He then continues:

"But the period of 40 years is nevertheless long enough to justify the anxious doubt as to whether in fact a reliable recollection of the events, and above all of the sayings of the Lord, still existed. Or had lack of understanding and deliberate intention, fanciful misrepresentation and fiction already accomplished their work of distortion and destruction, before the Evangelists undertook to protect the treasure from further decay and mutilation? Closing one's eyes to this doubt does not help, nor does the naive assertion that this was not the case, or the pious belief that God would not have permitted such damage to the teachings of Jesus, so necessary for us. Only thorough historical investigation and criticism will avail."

After giving examples from the Gospels to show how Jesus' sayings were changed and modified, Professor Weiss, in another passage of the same essay, expresses the following view:

"Considering these instances of misunderstanding and reshaping, we may well be overcome with painful regret that Jesus' words were not written down and passed on to us by His own hand, as is the case with Paul and so many other personalities who have led us to God. And we must earnestly ask: Were not many widely-diffused rays of His Light lost, because the mirror which was to hold them was too small and too dull? It can be safely assumed that some aspects of His Being have remained unknown to us because there was no observer who could have understood them. Many words would be lost because they did not call forth a response in the souls of these people. The selection preserved for us would be influenced by their narrow range of ideas, and certainly many a word was originally given a greater and deeper meaning than we read into it today."

So in connection with certain passages of the New Testament, the question as to what were the actual words of Jesus is really justified, and we must beware of asserting with regard to such doubtful texts that Jesus spoke in that way! In many matters Jesus did not speak as is explained and taught on the basis of false traditions. Take an example from Luke 14, 26: "If any man come to me, and hate not his father, and mother, and wife, and children, and brethren, and sisters, yea, and his own life also, he cannot be my disciple."

Jesus, Who is "Divine Love", would never have made discipleship dependent upon "hating" one's closest relations. In doing so He would have been inviting sin. And this immediately shows the absurdity of these transmitted words which Jesus is said to have uttered. He would have asked that too close personal ties should be avoided and that one's ego should not be placed in the foreground, so that His disciples might dedicate themselves without burden or restraint to the lofty task.

Equally inaccurate is the transmission about the Son of Man, with which we shall deal here in detail. At the end of His earthly activity Jesus gave His disciples the promise concerning the coming of the Son of Man. By the Son of Man He meant not Himself but another Person. The disciples did not understand this, and believed that Jesus Himself was the Son of Man, an assumption which was certainly understandable and excusable at the time, because they were living in imminent expectation of the Final Judgment and the return of Jesus.

Nevertheless – hardly had Jesus uttered what to mankind is the most significant prophecy – than the foundation was already laid for a very fateful error, which was passed on and finally incorporated in the Gospels. Hence they contain a number of incorrect or at least obscure phrases about the concept of the Son of Man, which Jesus in His simple and clear manner of expression would never have used.

2.

Clearly Jesus proclaims the coming of a second Envoy from God: "Nevertheless I tell you the truth; It is expedient for you that I go away: for if I go not away, the Comforter will not come unto you; but if I depart, I will send him unto you. And when he is come, he will reprove the world of sin, and of righteousness, and of judgment . . ." (John 16, 7-8).

"I have yet many things to say unto you, but ye cannot bear them now. Howbeit when he, the Spirit of truth, is come, he will guide you into all truth: for he shall not speak of himself . . ."

"He shall glorify me: for he shall receive of mine, and shall shew it unto you. All things that the Father hath are mine: therefore said I, that he shall take of mine, and shall shew it unto you" (John 16, 12-15).

"But the Comforter, which is the Holy Ghost, whom the Father will send in my name, he shall teach you all things, and bring all things to your remembrance, whatsoever I have said unto you" (John 14, 20).

"Whosoever therefore shall be ashamed of me and of my words . . . , of him also shall the Son of man be ashamed, when he cometh in the glory of his Father with the holy angels"

(Mark 8, 38). Just this last sentence is at once rendered unintelligible through the wrong assumption that Jesus and the Son of Man are one and the same Person.

All these words of Jesus refer to another Person, and not to the *impersonal* Power which Jesus had also promised His disciples: "And, behold, I send the promise of my Father upon you: but tarry ye in the city of Jerusalem, until ye be endued with power from on high" (Luke 24, 49).

This promise referred to the outpouring of Power through the Holy Spirit, an event which has been repeated every year at a definite time ever since the inception of Creation, for its maintenance. In those days the disciples experienced the fulfilment of this event at Whitsuntide, after being inwardly prepared for it through the grievous experience occasioned by the sudden and violent death of their Lord.

The activities which in His promise Jesus associates with the other Person, such as "to guide into all truth", "to preach", "to teach", "to bring to remembrance what Jesus has said", can only be carried out by a *person*, and therefore they necessitate a personal fulfilment.

In the explanatory notes on the New Testament, published by Otto v. Gerlach, Professor of Divinity and Court Chaplain (Berlin 1863), it is stated: "These words 'He shall not speak of himself' make sense only in regard to a person, not to an impersonal power or manifestation of God." In addition there is special reference to the importance of this great teaching of the Holy Scriptures regarding the Personality of the Holy Spirit, which was not nearly enough appreciated.

By the designations "Spirit of Truth", "Comforter" and "Holy Ghost" Jesus meant the Son of Man, Who will come to continue His Mission.

Not the least of His Works, by virtue of His High Office

— for He comes from God — will be to set right the errors in the transmissions and interpretations of Christ's words.

3.

And the Son of Man it is Who brings the World Judgment to men, because He is Justice. Whereas Jesus, Who works in Love, emphasised that He had not come to judge (John 12, 47). The judgeship was laid by God upon "Justice" in person, upon the Holy Spirit! His activity is manifested in the immutable Laws of Creation, and a transgression of these Laws is a sin against the Holy Spirit, which cannot be forgiven and must be expiated. Hence the words of the Bible, that sins against God and the Son of God can be forgiven, but not blasphemy against the Holy Ghost (Matthew 12, 31-32; Mark 3, 29).

How many earnest Christians have pondered in vain over the sense of these words, and have been oppressed by them, because they did not know the real meaning of the Holy Spirit. His Work lies in the adamantine and incorruptible Laws pulsating through Creation. To these also belongs the Law of Sowing and Reaping, which acts uniformly in the earthly as well as in the extra-earthly.

In the sense of this Law the thoughts, inner perception, conduct and actions of man are just as much seed as that which is placed in the earth, a spiritual seed which the one who has sown it must himself reap. No one else can gather the harvest of this seed for him, whether it be good or evil. Nor can Jesus do so, for He cannot change or evade the Laws of Creation, because He, as the Son of God, is just as subject to the Laws of His Father as are the creatures. For He stated explicitly that He would fulfil the Laws of His Father, and not destroy them (Matthew 5, 17).

Hence a man cannot forgive his neighbour the sins against the Holy Spirit. On the other hand, he has the power and also the right to forgive a wrong inflicted on him personally, and thus to prevent at the outset an evil reaction for the wrongdoer. It is in *this* sense that the words of Jesus: "Whose soever sins ye remit, they are remitted unto them...." (John 20, 23), should be understood.

Thus a man who, for instance, inflicts sorrow or harm on a fellow-man through his propensity for evil, can be pardoned immediately by the person in question, but only by him. In this way no evil threads of fate can develop out of this personal harm inflicted. The sinful propensity, however, which the wrongdoer bears within himself, and which was the motive for this deed, cannot be forgiven him by anyone. He must personally detach himself from it through true repentance, which is equivalent to a complete inner change for the good. If in the future he then heeds and obeys the Laws of the Holy Spirit instead of opposing them, the Grace of God which rests in these Laws will always be with him!

For the same reason Jesus was certainly able to pardon the abuses inflicted on Him personally, but was not in a position to prevent the grievous fate brought upon mankind through their rejection of His Mission and His Message from running its course, and from having to be resolved now in the World Judgment.

4.

The question of when the World Judgment will come is already answered for all those who look about them with open eyes.

We are standing in the midst of the great final reckoning of the Judgment Day or the Last Judgment. Daily we experience in ever-increasing intensity and frequency its effects, that is the consequences of the evil seed we have scattered in the world for thousands of years. The very frequency of events is a special feature of the World Judgment. It is the consequence of an undreamed-of, tremendous acceleration of everything that exists and is caused by the Divine Power which the Son of Man brings unchanged into Creation for the Judgment.

We need only for once contemplate the events which already for decades have brought mankind in ever-increasing measure unrest, horror, despair, distress and death, in order to recognise that an invisible power must stand behind them.

Whether it be the ever more violent dissensions, the schism, mutual distrust, wars, riots, the atomic arms race, political entanglements, economic difficulties, the unbelievable fate of individuals and masses, crimes, scandals and crises, or new diseases and epidemics, the natural catastrophes, as well as the unusual atmospheric conditions and temperatures over the whole earth.

Atomic power cannot cause the frequency and the unusual character of these happenings, but only the Divine Power anchored in Creation, against which the entire atomic power used by men, as well as man himself, is as nothing!

The attempt to control the swelling tide of chaos, or even to arrest it, is therefore doomed to failure. Man is simply flattened by the spiritual and earthly events, and is often confronted overnight by totally new situations and facts, with which he can cope only with the help of God.

Had men not long since forsaken their way to God, there need not be this terrible Judgment, in which everyone must receive his self-earned punishment for the sins he has nurtured in many earth-lives. For Jesus did not take all the sins of the world upon Himself through His death on the cross, which men regard as a necessary propitiatory sacrifice. The sins are still there, and come upon us like a gigantic burden in the World Judgment, which is carried out before our eyes, and which will strike every man at his time exactly according to the Law. "For whatsoever a man soweth, that shall he also reap" (Galatians 6, 7). This applies to *all* men, irrespective of their creed ...

<h2 style="text-align:center">5.</h2>

But let us once more return to the past and search out further words and sentences referring to the Son of Man, to His activity, His Mission and His coming. Perhaps such a retrospective view will bring a better understanding of the present.

In the Old Testament it is particularly Daniel and Isaiah who prophesy about the Son of Man. Isaiah calls Him by the name that God has given Him: "Imanuel!" (Isaiah 7, 14). This name has not been recognised in its true significance until now because men, without examination, generally adopted the view of the Evangelist Matthew that Jesus was Imanuel. This is one of those cases in which the Evangelist, in combining traditions, added his own erroneous view, naturally without evil intent. This error does not appear in the other Gospels.

Thus Matthew reports: "And she shall bring forth a son, and thou shalt call his name Jesus ..." (Matthew 1, 21), and subsequently likewise applies the prophecy of Isaiah (Isaiah 7, 14) "... and shall call his name Imanuel ..." (Matthew 1, 23) to the birth of the Son of God. This in spite of the fact that the two names are quite different, and that Jesus never called Himself Imanuel, nor was He ever so called; moreover He was never addressed by the name Son of Man.

In his wider vision Isaiah gives a noteworthy sign for the time of Imanuel: "Take counsel together, and it shall come to nought; speak the word, and it shall not stand: for God is with us" (Isaiah 8, 10). (Matthew 1, 23: "Emmanuel, which being interpreted is, God with us").

These words purport that the Son of Man is Executive Justice, Whose eternal and immutable Laws pulsate through Creation. Anything men do that is not in the sense of these Laws cannot last and must perish. But henceforth this will take place with uncanny acceleration, brought about through the Divine Power which the Son of Man brings unchanged to Creation for the Judgment. "For God is with us!" And wrong actions can no longer as before be concealed for a time, but must within a short time reveal themselves as such, visible to all. The increase in conferences which have come to nought, the empty promises, the perplexity, are signs of a wrong "counselling" and "speaking the word", and are part of the indications concerning the fulfilment of the prophecy.

A further sign of this is the appearance of the many false prophets (Matthew 24, 11). They are given this name because they promise to the seeking and erring human souls something which only the Son of Man has the power to grant! When they are there, the true Prophet will also step forth!

It is to Him that Paul also refers in the words: "For we know in part, and we prophesy in part. But when that which is perfect is come, then that which is in part shall be done away" (I Corinthians 13, 9-10). Only God is perfect, and His two Sons Jesus and Imanuel, Who both as a Part of God are eternally one with Him, and remain separate only in Their activity. For the Son of Man, Imanuel, also comes from God, as Jesus clearly states (John 16, 7-15), and is therefore according to earthly concepts a Son of God.

When Paul spoke these words, the disciples' Pentecostal experience was already past, so that his words cannot be referred to that event, as has been done.

An unknown prophet, whose prophecies are to be found in the Book of Enoch, also received deep insight into the spiritual happening and into the future of Imanuel, the Son of Man. We learn from this book that the Son of Man was already in being before the existence of Creation, and that He was at first hidden and only revealed to the chosen ones. But let us read the relevant passages from the prophecy itself:

"And I asked the angel who went with me and showed me all the hidden things, concerning that Son of Man, who He was, and whence He was and why He went with the Head of Days? And he answered and said unto me: 'This is the Son of Man who hath righteousness, with whom dwelleth righteousness, and who revealeth all the treasures of that which is hidden'" (Enoch 46, 2-3).

"And in that place I saw the fountain of righteousness which was inexhaustible; and around it were many fountains of wisdom; and all the thirsty drank of them and were filled with wisdom, and their dwellings were with the righteous and holy and elect. And at that hour that Son of Man was named in the presence of the Lord of Spirits, and His name before the Head of Days. Yea, before the sun and the signs were created, before the stars of the heaven were made, His name was named before the Lord of Spirits. He shall be a staff to the righteous whereon to stay themselves and not fall. And he shall be the light of the Gentiles, and the hope of those who are troubled of heart" (Enoch 48, 1-4).

"And the kings and the mighty and all who possess the earth shall bless and glorify and extol him who rules over all, who was hidden. For from the beginning the Son of Man was hidden, and the Most High preserved him in the presence of His might, and revealed him to the elect" (Enoch 62, 6-7).

"And there was great joy amongst them, and they blessed

and glorified and extolled ..., because the name of that Son of Man had been revealed unto them. And he sat on the throne of his glory, and the sum of judgment was given unto the Son of Man, and he caused the sinners to pass away and be destroyed from off the face of the earth, and those who have led the world astray" (Enoch 69, 26-27).

Presumably the Book of Enoch, which is not contained in our Bible, has been fully preserved only in the Ethiopian translation, after the Hebrew or Aramaic original was lost. Already at an early date the Book of Enoch was received into the Old Testament Canon of the Abyssinian Church. Thus in the seventeenth century it came to Europe as the Ethiopian Book of Enoch, as distinct from other, but only incomplete translations. It belongs to the so-called apocryphal (secret) writings, which according to Luther "cannot be considered equal to the Holy Scriptures, and yet are useful and good to read."

The tidings conveyed in the Book of Enoch, that the Son of Man was known by name even before the existence of Creation, are found again in the Proverbs of Solomon. There the Son of Man, Who is called by the name "Wisdom", says: "The Lord possessed me in the beginning of his way, before his works of old. I was set up from everlasting, from the beginning, or ever the earth was" (Proverbs 8, 22 and 23).

We learn further from these Proverbs of the nature of the task assigned by God to the Son of Man. We learn that He was "by him, as one brought up with him" (Proverbs 8, 22-31). His "Work", however, is Creation!

Finally the Son of Man says: "For whoso findeth me findeth life, and shall obtain favour of the Lord. But he that sinneth against me wrongeth his own soul: all they that hate me love death" (Proverbs 8, 35-36). The words "that sinneth against me" are equivalent to the sin against the Holy Spirit, which has already been explained.

6.

These references are of course not exhaustive. Many another prophecy apart from the Bible refers to the coming of a great helper for humanity. The holy tidings of this were not given only to the Jewish people, although for the Jews in particular they have an especially fateful meaning.

For in those days most of them, in their expectation of the Messiah, rejected Jesus as the Son of God, although at that time they bore within them the greatest potentiality for spiritual understanding, and had therefore been singled out as the chosen people for the incarnation of the Envoy of God. For them, too, the last opportunity to redeem the guilt of their former failure has come if they recognise the Son of Man, Imanuel, as the Messiah foretold by their prophets, and so longingly awaited for thousands of years!

The Son of Man could not yet come at that time. He was in the midst of His extensive preparation for His great Mission, a preparation lasting thousands of years according to human conceptions. This however was not intended until the time of the Cosmic Turning-Point, which is taking place at the present time in accordance with the unalterable Laws of Development, and is simultaneously connected with the World Judgment.

In the meantime men would have sunk into night and darkness as a result of their volition being constantly turned away from the Light. As speedy help was imperative, God the Father in His inconceivable Love sent Jesus to be incarnated in the Gross Material World, to re-establish directly the connection with God, which mankind had long since severed – this for the sake of the few who still carried within them a spark of longing for the Light. It was a Divine Act of Emergency, which resulted in Jesus' coming to earth without great preparations, and after completing His Mission, although remaining personal, He again had to return wholly to the Father as the Inborn Son (John 16, 28), and as Ruler in the Divine Kingdom; for "His Kingdom is not of this world" (John 18, 36). The Kingdom of the Son of Man, on the other hand, is the entire Creation, including the World of Matter. From the beginning He was firmly linked with His Work as the "Upbuilder" of Creation, so that He remains "Outborn" as the Eternal Mediator between God and mankind "... that he may abide with you forever" (John 14, 16).

For this reason He bears the name "Son of Man", not perhaps because He was to be born of earthman. This could not be the case, for the simple reason that His earthly birth was not originally intended. According to prophecy the Son of Man was to have appeared for the Judgment "coming in a cloud", that is, outside the earthly sphere. The change in this was a further great Deed of Love on the part of the Creator, occasioned by men's continual failure.

Already by the end of the earthly activity of Jesus it was apparent that mankind would not recognise His Mission. This did not consist in coming to earth to permit Himself to be murdered, but in bringing the Truth, the Word of God, so that in the Word of Truth men could find and tread the way to the forgiveness of sins and redemption.

And so it could be foreseen that the great majority of men would not follow the way shown to them, and would persist in their spiritual indolence. Their final doom could then no longer be arrested; for the few who were striving upwards had not the strength to prevent the fall into the abyss.

Hence the Son of Man could only completely help, and

save man and the earth from total destruction, by bringing them His Message personally. Only thus was He in a position to reach spiritually those earthmen who were still of good will, and through the Word of God, which He brought in earthly form, to throw out to them in their desperate straits a sure lifeline from their immediate proximity.

7.

That this stupendous event has already taken place on earth without being recognised by the majority of Christians, can be attributed in part to the faulty transmission of the concept of the Son of Man, hardly noticed until now, and to the fact that human ideas and expectations are so little in harmony with Divine fulfilments.

Thus, in exact accordance with the prophecy of Jesus, the appearance of the Son of Man took place at an hour when men were not thinking about it (Matthew 24, 44)! Outwardly a man among men, recognised only by a small number of seekers, the Son of Man dwelt on earth in Abd-ru-shin, and left it again after a lengthy path of suffering, abuse and disappointments.

In the Grail Message "In the Light of Truth" He brought to human spirits in this world and the beyond the new Knowledge of Creation. In this the Teaching of Christ is fully and completely confirmed and presented as it actually is, free from all faulty transmissions, and free from all human additions.

At the same time the Grail Message is the evidence which reveals the Son of Man as Envoy of God. For the earnest seeker it is written therein: "He should examine *the words* within himself and let them come to life without heeding the speaker. Otherwise he derives no benefit from them."

To human beings, and especially to adherents of the Christian faiths, it is so completely strange that the Son of Man now brings a Grail Message and calls Himself Abd-ru-shin, that most of them refuse to concern themselves with it. And once more the words of Jesus sound in our ear: "Nevertheless, when the Son of man cometh, shall He find faith on the earth?" (Luke 18, 8).

They justify their rejection by saying that Jesus never spoke of the Grail. But they do not recollect His words: "I have yet many things to say unto you, but ye cannot bear them now. Howbeit when he, the Spirit of truth, is come, he will guide you into all truth" (John 16, 12-13).

To this Truth belongs the knowledge of the Grail, whose actual existence is confirmed and explained in the Grail Message. The Holy Grail is a Vessel in the Grail Castle in the highest Spiritual Realm, in Primordial Creation, at the border to the Divine Kingdom. From this Vessel, in eternal rhythm from the beginning of Creation, through the mediation of the Son of Man, the Holy Spirit, the streams of Living Water flow into Creation for its sustenance and continuance. "I am Alpha and Omega, the beginning and the end. I will give unto him that is athirst of the fountain of the water of life freely," so reads the promise of the Son of Man in the Revelation of John (21, 6). The "fountain of the water of life", however, is the Holy Grail!

Already from time to time in the course of thousands of years tidings of the existence of the Grail in the Spiritual Realm have come to earth, but they have been rendered all too earthly by the human intellect, so that the true source remained unclear and clouded, and the genuine longing for the exalted and pure that lies in the Grail could not arise in the souls of men.

114

Unfamiliar as this new knowledge may appear at first to seeking man, he cannot avoid occupying himself with it; because the time is simply ripe for it.

The Cosmic Turning-Point, with its cataclysmic and irresistible events, has already begun. And with every great turning-point, which is always related to Creation's state of maturity at the time, there is also linked an extension of the Knowledge of Creation. At the present Turning-Point the new Knowledge has been personally revealed by the Son of Man, Imanuel, in fulfilment of the Words of the Son of God, Jesus: "When, however, the Son of Man cometh . . ."!

With this Turning-Point the promise of Jesus, which He gave at that time in regard to His own coming as a consolation to His people ". . . I will come again . . ." (John 14, 3), also became a reality. His presence in Creation at the time of the Last Judgment, through a process of radiation closely connected with the Son of Man, Imanuel, is the fulfilment of His return! This process, however, will always remain incomprehensible to the human spirit!

The Message of the Son of Man is now the last Divine Revelation for mankind, which closes a long evolution of the human spirit-germ into a spirit that has become conscious of itself, and initiates a new great epoch in the Light of Truth, beginning with the long and ardently desired Millennium, which all those who are pure in heart may enter.

Let the human spirit bow in humility before the infinite Wisdom and Goodness of its Lord and God!

Further works from our publishers:

In the Light of Truth

The Grail Message of Abd-ru-shin

Volume I   "Free yourself from all darkness!"
               236 pages

Volume II   "Now stride upwards vigorously!"
               484 pages

Volume III   "Expand your knowledge!"
               512 pages

A special book, which clearly answers the unsolved problems of human existence. The vast knowledge mediated in its pages leads the earnestly-seeking reader, who weighs and examines objectively, out of all the chaos of the present-day confusion and distortion, to clear recognitions.

This book commands attention by its forceful language, by the clarity of its thoughts and by the setting right of distorted concepts, unmistakably and sometimes severely but irrefutably explained.

The Laws in which the entire Creation came into being and exists are plainly set forth, the World Happening is interpreted in its true significance, and man's responsibility before God and his fellow-men is revealed and explained. Thus to him who opens himself to these recognitions is restored the indestructible inner security of his personality.

Verlag der Stiftung Gralsbotschaft
Lenzhalde 15, D-7000 Stuttgart 1

Further writings by Abd-ru-shin:

Selected Lectures
This booklet contains a few lectures selected from the Work
"In the Light of Truth", The Grail Message by Abd-ru-shin,
which show the importance of this unique Work.

The Ten Commandments of God and the
Lord's Prayer
In this book (pocket size) Abd-ru-shin gives an explanation of
the Ten Commandments and the Lord's Prayer, in order to
make them once more fully understandable to present-day
mankind.

Questions and Answers
In this book Abd-ru-shin answers questions with which he has
been approached during the years 1924 to 1937, from all
spheres of life and knowledge.

Prayers
Given to mankind by Abd-ru-shin

Verlag der Stiftung Gralsbotschaft
Lenzhalde 15, D-7000 Stuttgart 1

Publications of
The Grail Message Foundation

These publications deal with fundamental and decisive problems of our time, in order to fathom their original causes, and
at the same time to indicate a way to overcome the difficulties
of shaping our lives aright.

Published to date:

Booklet 1   The Messages of God

Booklet 2   The Son of God – Birth and Trial of Jesus

Booklet 3   Trip into Illusion

Pocket Book 1 The World, as it could be!

Pocket Book 2 Knowledge for the World of Tomorrow!

Pocket Book 3 What lies behind it...!

Verlag der Stiftung Gralsbotschaft
Lenzhalde 15, D-7000 Stuttgart 1.